gorgeousvegetables

Annie Bell

gorgeousvegetables

with photographs by Chris Alack

Kyle Books

This edition published in 2010 by Kyle Books
An imprint of Kyle Cathie Limited
www.kylecathie.com

Distributed by National Book Network
4501 Forbes Blvd., Suite 200
Lanham, MD 20706
Phone: (800) 462 6420

First published by Kyle Cathie Limited 2009

ISBN 978-1-906868-24-6

The Library of Congress Cataloging-in-Publication Data is available on file.

10 9 8 7 6 5 4 3 2 1

Editor: Suzanna de Jong
Design: pinkstripedesign@hotmail.com
Copy Editor: Annie Lee
Proofreader: Stephanie Evans
Indexer: Ann Kingdom
Americanizer: Elizabeth Brais
Photographer: Chris Alack
Home Economist: Kim Morphew
Prop Stylist: Sue Radcliffe
Production: Sha Huxtable

Color reproduction: Colourscan, Singapore
Printed and bound in Singapore by Star Standard Industries Pty Ltd

contents

introduction

The greens of my childhood were a narrow concept: leafy cabbages that were normaly boiled, with the leftovers turned into bubble and squeak, which was the best thing. We gobbled them up because we were told to, with almost every dinner at certain times of the year. But this is harking back to the Sixties and Seventies, long before all things green had become desirable, while today the term "greens" is a fond one that has come to mean any vegetable, not just cabbage leaves, though these too have advanced beyond all recognition.

A large part of the advance has been to do with the way we cook. Looking back as recently as even ten years ago,

to when I first wrote a book on vegetables, pretty much the only roasted vegetables in it were parsnips and potatoes, and salads had yet to blossom into the big blowsy affairs we have become accustomed to seeing piled high in the windows of glam cafés. Where once they were a slap on the wrist after a few days' indulgence, today they are actually used to lure us in. I have a complete passion for green salads, hence an entire chapter is devoted to them. One of my favorite standby suppers revolves around roast chicken and small crispy potatoes, which leaves lots of time to spend whisking up a salad dressing and washing and drying a selection of green leaves, for wiping the plate clean. And there is little better way of rounding off any mealtime than with a sliver of goat cheese or mature Cheddar and a pile of crisp, lightly dressed salad greens.

But it's not all austerity—gratins possess the essential yummy factor, with their crisp edges and gooey cheese. And there is a chapter on vegetable main courses, filled with lovely tarts—miniature pizzettas made with puff pastry, deep, lightly set creamy quiches, and hearty pies. I also experiment with grains more and more, like spelt and quinoa; with us since time immemorial, they have acquired a new lease of life. In fact, I suspect if we really wanted to predict the next grain fad, we need look no further than a pharaoh's tomb, since the fashion at the moment is for rediscovery.

The opening chapter of the book, however, is a rather more recent trip back in time, and one I personally find

nostalgic: a medley of dips. I adore dips, which were as central to my childhood as bubble and squeak, but ultimately they're as contemporary as what you dunk in them. As fridge raiding goes it doesn't get much healthier, and these make a great standby.

The chapter on potatoes spans all our favorite ways of serving them: lots of salads, sautéed, baked, and stuffed, and little is more comforting than when they form the basis of a soup with a good chicken stock.

As well as the type of dish, the choice of vegetables is getting better and better. Some twenty years ago tomatoes were "standard," perfectly round red fruits a little bigger than a plum, with nothing very thrilling to recommend either their appearance or their flavor. Whereas now, come summer, we are spoiled with cherry tomatoes in sunny shades of orange and red, some cocktail-sized and on the vine, baby plums, and others little larger than a raisin. At the other end of the scale there are big beefsteak tomatoes dripping with juices,

and wonderful heirloom varieties with amorphic shapes and pleated tops. With a little hunting we can amass a stunning collection of types to feast on.

Then there are greens themselves, which go so much further than boiling. The choice has been broadened out to include cavolo nero, a bubbly dark green leaf with a real depth of flavor, not dissimilar from our own derided kale, that takes on a new dimension when bought in the same fashion—on the stalk—and stripped off it. But my real new love is long-stem broccoli. While spring has long been a treat of a season for purple sprouting broccoli with its sweet flavor and tender stalks, we are now rarely without some variety of long-stem broccoli during the remainder of the year. It's at its best blanched, brushed with olive oil, and grilled on a grill pan, which opens up the way for all manner of wonderful salads where it can be married with other gutsy ingredients like lentils and dates.

And next up is chicory, a vegetable we are just on the cusp of discovering, having long regarded the pale green *chicons* so appreciated in the Netherlands, Belgium, and France as being strangely bitter. They are sublime tossed with olive oil and thrown into a hot oven, and make for delicious salads with sweet mustardy dressings. Any food with an edge, be it sour, salty, sweet, or hot, can be married with foods offering the opposite. These leaves lap up blue cheese, salty bacon and hams, and sweet ingredients such as dried figs and prunes come to life. We seem at last to be taking the red varieties on board too.

Bringing all these lovely vegetables together, there is probably no more pivotal an arrival on these shores than extra virgin olive oil. Those poor pioneering spirits of the Fifties and earlier in following their heart to the Mediterranean were forced to rely on small bottles of olive oil (not even extra

virgin) from the pharmacist once they returned home, where it was normally sold for medicinal purposes. By the time I started cooking in the Eighties extra virgin olive oil was a given, and if I count the number of recipes in the book that rely on it, we are approaching some eighty percent. I'm not sure where greens would be today in its absence.

Even though this book isn't strictly vegetarian, any meat or fish is incidental, and if you are someone who normally eschews them you will still find plenty to please. The recipes are more than anything a celebration of the produce itself. Farmers' markets and specialized shops are glorious hunting grounds for really good veggies—big boxes piled high with soil-crusted roots, cabbages with snails clinging inside their outer leaves, carrots and beets with their tops attached, a general sense of things having only recently been pulled from a field, casting in their turn a general sense of well-being that comes with eating lots of gorgeous vegetables.

dips

For those of us who can remember the Seventies, dips will be forever entwined with full-length, orange-check evening dresses. They're very "In The Lounge" with Andy Williams. In fact, one of my earliest memories of party time as a child was of my mother's "dip," a triumph of its time. A couple of packages of Philadelphia Cream Cheese thrown in a blender with a little chopped onion or shallot, a squeeze of lemon juice, and enough milk to give it a dipping consistency, liberally dusted with cayenne pepper. "Chips and Dip" were fantastically good and just as bad for you.

Several decades down the line, judging from the refrigerated sections of supermarkets, we still can't get enough, though inevitably they have evolved, or rather the dunkers have. Scooped straight from the tub with some cherry tomatoes or slivers of carrot, dips today are one of the healthiest of snacks and will lure the most reluctant veg-o-phobe, in the same way that melted chocolate will convince the fruit-shy to eat their apples.

Crudités tend to taste better the thinner you cut them; hard and crisp with a little bite soothed by a big dollop of a creamy dip seems to cut the right balance. And younger fare better than old—baby fennel bulbs, slender young carrots, and celery hearts. Or look to the Lebanese, who make a fine art of raw vegetables at the start of every meal. A plate of peppers, tomatoes, scallions, baby cucumbers, a half lettuce, and some radishes will arrive with beads of water clinging, and with it a selection of pickles.

Dust dips with a little crushed cumin or toasted coriander seed and give them a drizzle of oil, and they are at the ready for a more elegant selection of eats. You can play on the Greek mezze inherent in them by serving a couple of dips with marinated olives, a block of feta to chip away at, and some warm pita bread cooked on a grill pan until they're branded with a golden lattice pattern.

This is something like a baba ghanoush, without the raw rasp of garlic it normally carries in its wake. Pomegranate offsets the faint bitterness of the eggplants, as do the toasted almonds, and it's altogether gentler.

eggplant purée with pomegranate and almonds

2 pounds eggplant (3 large ones)

4 slices of day-old white bread, crusts removed, torn into pieces

1 garlic clove, peeled and coarsely chopped

1 tablespoon red wine vinegar

5 tablespoons extra virgin olive oil, plus extra to serve

sea salt, black pepper

1 tablespoon lemon juice

seeds from ½ pomegranate

1 tablespoon toasted almond flakes

Serves 6

Preheat the oven to 425°F. Prick the eggplants all over and bake for 25 minutes, until the skin is wrinkled and darker. While they are cooking, soak the bread in water for 5 minutes, then squeeze out the water, though it shouldn't be too dry. Place the bread in a food processor with the garlic and vinegar and process to a smooth cream. With the motor running, add the olive oil.

Skin the eggplants and thickly slice the cooked flesh. Place it in a sieve and press out as much juice as possible. Add the flesh to the bread mixture in the food processor and purée together, adding some seasoning. Transfer the purée to a shallow bowl. You can prepare the recipe to this point in advance.

To serve, drizzle a swirl of oil and the lemon juice on top of the purée. Scatter the pomegranate seeds and almond flakes on top.

These could just as well be served alone as together, but they do complement each other especially well, trailing the Provençal Riviera in their wake. You can serve any mixture of crudités—fine slivers of celery heart, red and yellow cherry tomatoes, and strips of pepper. Radishes too: try to buy these by the bunch, as their foliage is the best indicator of their freshness. Long, slim breakfast radishes are the tastiest of all.

crushed goat cheese and anchoïade

Crushed Goat Cheese

8 ounces medium-mature goat cheese,
    rind removed
3 tablespoons extra virgin olive oil
black pepper
a few slivers of scallions,
    white and green parts

Anchoïade

4 garlic cloves, peeled
16 anchovy fillets in oil
15 green olives, pitted
⅔ cup extra virgin olive oil
1 teaspoon sherry vinegar

Serves 6

To make the crushed goat cheese, crumble the cheese into a bowl and mash to a coarse paste with the olive oil and black pepper. Serve in a small bowl with a few fine slivers of scallion scattered over it.

To make the anchoïade, place the garlic, anchovies, and olives in a food processor and reduce to a coarse purée. Add the olive oil and vinegar and process at high speed until you have a smooth paste.

As the season for fava beans progresses their skins toughen and the flesh becomes that much more mealy, and here the purée is sieved, making it a good one for midsummer. But equally it's a real quickie should you have a package of frozen fava beans hanging around the freezer. Some cooked tail-on shrimp and quail's eggs would make delicious dunkers, as does warm pita bread. Alternatively you could spoon it on top of crispy, fried sea bass fillets by way of a sauce.

spicy fava bean dip

1½ pounds fresh or frozen fava beans

¾ teaspoon chopped medium hot
    green chile

1 level teaspoon ground cumin

1 teaspoon paprika, plus extra
    for dusting

1 garlic clove, peeled and chopped

sea salt, black pepper

7 tablespoons extra virgin olive oil,
    plus extra to serve

juice of 1 lemon

Serves 6

Cook the fava beans in boiling water for 8 minutes if fresh, 3–4 minutes if frozen. Purée them in a food processor with the chile, cumin, paprika, garlic, and some seasoning, trickling in the olive oil and lemon juice. Pass through a sieve into a bowl and serve drizzled with olive oil and sprinkled with paprika.

This sweet and addictive dip may find fans among you for its absence of garlic and raw onion, though more to the point it is low-fat. I'd think in terms of a little salad of grated zucchini and some caper berries alongside, or a few slices of salami rolled up and skewered with a cocktail stick, as well as some crackers or bread.

red pepper mezze

6 red peppers
1 slice of coarse-textured white
  bread, toasted
⅓ cup pine nuts, toasted
2 tablespoons Greek yogurt
a squeeze of lemon juice
sea salt, black pepper
1 tablespoon each of chopped
  fresh cilantro and mint, plus extra
  to serve

Serves 6–8

Roast the peppers for 20 minutes at 425°F, then place them in a bowl, cover, and leave to cool. Reduce the toast to crumbs in a food processor, then process the pine nuts to coarse crumbs. Skin and de-seed the peppers and purée in the food processor.

Transfer the purée to a bowl and stir in the breadcrumbs, pine nuts, yogurt, lemon juice, some seasoning, and the herbs. Leave to stand for an hour or so before eating, and serve with a few extra herbs scattered on top.

This dip plays on the better nature of pumpkins and butternut squash to reduce to a silken purée; they also lap up spices and other aromatics, which makes them a great medium for all things Middle Eastern. Olives and a sharp sheep cheese go down well here too.

pumpkin dip

1¼ pounds butternut squash
  or pumpkin flesh
juice of 1 lemon
6 tablespoons extra virgin olive oil,
  plus extra to serve
1 teaspoon harissa
1 garlic clove, peeled and crushed
  to a paste
1 teaspoon ground coriander
sea salt, black pepper
coarsely chopped fresh cilantro
  (optional)

Serves 6

Steam the squash or pumpkin flesh for 15 minutes until tender. Transfer to a bowl and coarsely mash, then combine with the lemon juice, olive oil, harissa, garlic, ground coriander, sea salt, and black pepper. Transfer to a clean bowl, drizzle with a little more olive oil, and scatter with chopped cilantro, if desired.

Dyed a sunny yellow courtesy of a pinch of saffron, this is a little more thrilling than ordinary tzatziki, which are available as ready-made tubs in the refrigerated section of supermarkets and are one of the healthiest dips.

saffron tzatziki

a pinch of saffron filaments
   (approx. 20)
1 tablespoon extra virgin olive oil,
   plus a little extra to serve
1 teaspoon white wine vinegar
1 cup Greek yogurt
½ teaspoon superfine sugar
sea salt
½ cucumber
1 heaping teaspoon finely chopped
   shallot
1 heaping teaspoon finely sliced mint,
   plus a little extra to serve
cayenne pepper

Serves 4

Grind the saffron in a pestle and mortar and infuse in a teaspoon of boiling water for 15 minutes. Whisk the olive oil, vinegar, yogurt, saffron infusion, sugar, and a little salt together in a bowl. Peel the cucumber, quarter lengthways, remove the seeds, and dice the flesh very finely by first slicing the quarters into thin strips. Add the cucumber, shallot, and mint to the bowl, and taste for seasoning. To serve, decorate with a swirl of olive oil, a little finely sliced mint, and a dusting of cayenne pepper.

With its Norman roots this dip has subtly changing textures, and relies on an aromatic mature goat cheese with a dash of Calvados to bring out its character. You want something that's slightly runny at the edges while chalky within. A simpler aside to the salad that lends itself to being a little appetizer or light lunch would be chicory leaves and halved walnuts, and thick slices of sourdough bread.

creamy goat cheese

Creamy Goat Cheese

5 ounces young fresh goat cheese

7 ounces mature goat cheese, rind removed

3 tablespoons sour cream

3 teaspoons cider vinegar

1 tablespoon Calvados or brandy

½ garlic clove, crushed to a paste

1 tablespoon finely chopped fresh chives, plus a few extra to serve

Salad

1 level teaspoon Dijon mustard

sea salt, black pepper

1 tablespoon walnut oil

1 tablespoon peanut oil

2 heads of chicory, base trimmed

¼ cup walnuts, finely chopped

Serves 4

Mash the goat cheeses and sour cream together in a bowl to a textured cream. Blend 1 teaspoon of the vinegar, the Calvados, and crushed garlic into the goat cheese, and stir in the chives. Transfer to a clean bowl, cover, and chill until required. The recipe can be prepared to this point in advance.

Make the salad as close to the time of eating as possible to avoid the chicory discoloring. Whisk the remaining vinegar with the mustard and some seasoning in a bowl, then whisk in the oils until the dressing is thick and creamy. Discard the outer chicory leaves, halve the heads lengthways, and cut out the central core. Finely slice the leaves into long strips and toss with the dressing in a bowl, then mix in the walnuts. Serve the salad with a large dollop of creamed goat cheese and a few chives scattered on top.

An excellent use for the last of a big hunk of Stilton, which makes it a good one around Christmas; the slightly dry cheese towards the rind that gets left until the end is just as tasty as the center, if not so appetizing to behold. I first encountered sherried Stilton as a tapa in Seville, which may provide some inspiration for how to eat it other than with this crisp little salad—it's heaven with little warm crusty white rolls and a small glass of fino sherry.

sherried stilton

Sherried Stilton

10½ ounces Stilton (weight excluding rind)

4 tablespoons medium sherry

Salad

1 pound cooked and peeled beet, cut into slim wedges

2 tablespoons extra virgin olive oil

2 teaspoons sherry vinegar

2 teaspoons lemon juice

sea salt, black pepper

pale green celery leaves from 2 heads, sliced lengthways if large

3 tablespoons pecan nuts, thinly sliced

wafer-thin slices of toast to serve

Serves 6

Coarsely crumble the Stilton into a bowl. Pour over the sherry and gently mash to a textured purée.

To make the salad, toss the beet with the oil, vinegar, lemon juice, and some seasoning in a bowl, then mix in three-quarters of the celery leaves and nuts. Divide the salad between six side plates and scatter the remaining celery leaves and nuts over it. Place 1 tablespoon of the cheese to the side and serve with toast slices.

Alternatively place the salad in a salad bowl, and the cheese in another bowl, and leave everyone to help themselves.

Harry's Bar refers to this as a pâté, but as it has a dippy kind of consistency it's game for slivers of nascent vegetables and shards of toasted flatbread, as well as being yummy dolloped on toast. It's a particularly useful one, given how many of us have a couple of cans of tuna sitting in the back of the pantry, and it's comforting to know you can create a halfway glamorous offering at the drop of a hat.

harry's bar tuna dip

14 ounces of canned tuna in
   water, well drained
1 tablespoon lemon juice
1 tablespoon brandy
sea salt, black pepper
3 tablespoons mayonnaise
cayenne pepper
breadsticks, radishes, and caper
   berries to serve

Serves 6

Mix the tuna in a food processor with the lemon juice, brandy, and some seasoning. Transfer the fish to a bowl and beat in the mayonnaise. Serve dusted with cayenne pepper, accompanied by the breadsticks, radishes, and caper berries.

roasted vegetables

I love the sheer simplicity of this Barbara Cartland pink soup, it's true to the vegetable. While boiled beets can be insipid and unfriendly, and to me recalls Russian state-run hotels back in the days when the red flag was flying, roasting them concentrates their flavor and brings out their sweetness, as does a little lemon.

roasted beet and lemon soup with watercress

2 pounds good-sized raw beets
3 tablespoons extra virgin olive oil
sea salt, black pepper
1 strip of lemon zest, removed with a
    potato peeler, and 1 tablespoon
    lemon juice
sour cream and coarsely chopped
    watercress, or a sprig, to serve

Serves 4

Preheat the oven to 475°F. Without peeling the beets, trim the tops and bottoms of shoots and roots, and quarter or cut into wedges. Arrange these in a large roasting dish, pour over the olive oil, season, and roast for 40 minutes until tender, stirring halfway through.

Purée the contents of the roasting pan in batches with 3½ cups of water, the lemon zest and juice, and plenty of seasoning. Pass through a sieve into a saucepan and gently reheat. Serve with a spoonful of sour cream and lots of chopped watercress, or a sprig on top.

Dished up while the potatoes and onions are still warm, the horseradish sauce languidly melts over the top.

roasted sweet potatoes with horseradish

2½ pounds small, orange-fleshed sweet
　　potatoes, peeled and quartered
　　lengthways, halved if long
extra virgin olive oil
1 level tablespoon onion seeds or thyme
　　(use more), cumin, or caraway seeds
sea salt, black pepper
2 large red onions, peeled, halved, and
　　thinly sliced
2 tablespoons finely grated fresh
　　horseradish, or 2 teaspoons
　　prepared sauce
⅔ cup sour cream
watercress to serve 4

Serves 4

Preheat the oven to 475°F. Toss the sweet potatoes in a large bowl with 3 tablespoons of olive oil, the onion seeds, and some seasoning, then place into a large roasting dish that will hold them in a crowded single layer and roast for 30–40 minutes, stirring halfway through. At the same time, toss the onions in a large bowl with a couple of tablespoons of oil, then spread these out on a baking sheet and roast for 15–17 minutes, until golden and caramelized, stirring halfway through. Blend the horseradish with the sour cream and a little salt.

Mix the onions into the sweet potatoes. Toss the watercress with 1 tablespoon of olive oil and a little salt. Serve the potatoes with the horseradish spooned on top, and a pile of watercress. The vegetables are just as good eaten cold, in which case forgo the sauce.

This is a great way of roasting red onions. They turn out crispy at the edges and intensely sweet, and they're gorgeous scattered over pretty much any salad or stuffed into a sandwich with some rare roast beef or a chicken kebab.

salad of beets, roasted red onions, and arugula

1½ pounds red onions, peeled, halved, and thickly sliced

6 tablespoons extra virgin olive oil

2 teaspoons fresh thyme leaves

sea salt, black pepper

1 teaspoon balsamic vinegar

⅓ cup peeled hazelnuts

1 pound cooked and peeled beets, halved and cut into wedges

3 tablespoons coarsely snipped fresh chives

a handful of arugula leaves

Serves 6

Preheat the oven to 400°F. Scatter the onion slices over the base of a roasting dish in a crowded single layer and drizzle over 4 tablespoons of olive oil. Scatter over the thyme and a little salt, and roast for 40–45 minutes until golden, stirring halfway through. Drizzle over the vinegar and leave to cool. At the same time as roasting the onions, scatter the hazelnuts over the base of a small baking dish, toast in the oven for 10 minutes until golden, then remove and leave to cool.

Toss the beets, onion, and hazelnuts in a large salad bowl with another couple of tablespoons of oil and season. Mix in the chives and arugula leaves.

Penne pasta and shavings of Parmesan are also particularly fine with
roasted butternut, in which case a dash of balsamic vinegar will do well
in lieu of the harissa.

roasted squash and lentils with harissa dressing

2 butternut squash (approx. 1¾ pound
  each)
7 tablespoons extra virgin olive oil
sea salt, black pepper
7 ounces French green lentils
2 large red onions, peeled, halved, and
  thinly sliced
2–3 cups butter lettuce or bibb lettuce

Dressing
2 teaspoons harissa
2 teaspoons lemon juice
2 tablespoons extra virgin olive oil

Serves 4–6

Heat the oven to 400°F. Slice the top and bottom off the squash, then
halve them and cut off the skin. Quarter the bulbs to remove the seeds and
slice these sections into wedges. Halve the remaining cylindrical trunks
lengthways and slice ½ inch thick. Arrange the squash in a roasting dish
in a crowded single layer. Drizzle over 3 tablespoons of olive oil, season,
and roast for 1 hour. Turn the squash after 30 minutes, and again after
45 minutes.

About 20 minutes after putting the squash in to roast, bring a medium-sized
pan of water to a boil. Add the lentils and cook for about 25 minutes until
just tender, then drain into a sieve.

Toss the onions with 2 tablespoons of oil, scatter over the base of a large
roasting dish, and put into the oven when the squash have been cooking for
35 minutes to cook for the rest of the time. Stir them halfway through.

Add the onions and lentils to the pan with the squash and pour over the
remaining oil. Scatter over some salt and gently turn, using a spatula.

Whisk the harissa and lemon juice together in a bowl, then whisk in the oil.
Pour this over the salad leaves in a bowl, and serve the salad piled on top
of the squash and lentils. The squash and lentils can also be served at room
temperature, in which case dress the salad at the last minute.

two ways with mushrooms

Divine as Portabello mushrooms are, here you want the standard flat-cap ones that are that little bit deeper.

grilled manchego-stuffed mushrooms

3 ounces sourdough or other
   open-textured white bread
   (weight excluding crusts)
12 flat-cap mushrooms, stalks
   trimmed level with caps
8 tablespoons extra virgin olive oil

sea salt, black pepper
12 thin triangles of Manchego
   (approx. 4½ oz excluding rind)
12 fresh sage leaves

Serves 6

Preheat the oven to 425°F. Break up the bread and chop to coarse crumbs in a food processor. Arrange the mushrooms in 2 roasting dishes. Drizzle over 3 tablespoons of oil and season them. Lay one Manchego slice in the center of each mushroom, breaking off the tip if necessary so it lies within the edges of the mushroom. Place a sage leaf on top, then drizzle over another 3 tablespoons of oil. Toss the breadcrumbs with the remaining 2 tablespoons of oil and scatter over. Bake for 15 minutes, until the cheese is crusty and golden at the edges and the breadcrumbs are toasted and crisp.

The ham wrapped around the mushrooms turns papery crisp in the oven, sealing in the moussey goat cheese and all those satanically dark mushroom juices.

portabello mushrooms wrapped in prosciutto with goat cheese

8 portabello mushrooms
extra virgin olive oil
sea salt, black pepper
8 ounces chèvre log, rind
    removed, sliced
8 slices of prosciutto

Serves 4

Preheat the oven to 400°F. Cut the stalks off the mushrooms level with the caps. Brush the mushrooms on both sides with olive oil and season them. Divide the goat cheese between the caps and wrap each mushroom in a slice of prosciutto, placing it over the mushroom cap, and tucking the pieces underneath. Arrange the mushrooms in a roasting dish cup side up, drizzle over a couple of tablespoons of oil, and bake for 25 minutes, until the prosciutto has begun to crisp and the cheese is melted and golden at the edges.

It is increasingly easy to get hold of yellow or golden beets, which have an excellent flavor and cook up in exactly the same fashion as purple ones, and they make a fine change. You could also stir in some chopped leafy herbs—flat-leaf parsley, chives, or chervil—here.

grilled broccoli and beets with lentils

1½ pounds small uncooked beets

4 small sprigs of fresh rosemary

extra virgin olive oil

juice of 1½ lemons

3 garlic cloves, peeled and crushed
  to a paste

sea salt, black pepper

½ pound French green lentils

1 pound purple sprouting or tenderstem
  broccoli, trimmed

Serves 6

Preheat the oven to 475°F. Trim the shoots of the beets to within ½ inch of the top, but leave the whiskery tail intact, and give them a good scrub. Place them in a large bowl. Pull off half the rosemary needles and scatter these and the twigs over the beets. Toss with 4 tablespoons of olive oil, the juice of 1 lemon, the garlic, and some seasoning. Place into a roasting dish and roast for 30–40 minutes, until the skins are golden and puffy and the insides tender, turning them halfway through. Leave to stand for about 10 minutes.

At the same time as roasting the beets, bring a large pan of water to a boil. Add the lentils and cook for 20–25 minutes until tender, then drain them into a sieve. Bring another pan of water to a boil, add the broccoli, and cook for 3 minutes, then drain and leave for a few minutes for the surface moisture to evaporate. Heat a ridged grill pan over medium heat. Toss the broccoli in a large bowl with a couple of tablespoons of oil and some seasoning, and grill in two or three batches for 2–3 minutes each side until golden.

Trim the top and bottom of the beets, and quarter or slice into wedges. Place them in a large shallow serving dish and scatter the lentils on top. Pour over the roasting oil with another 4 tablespoons of oil, the remaining lemon juice, and some seasoning, and gently toss. Mix in the broccoli. This is delicious at any temperature, but if serving it cold you may need to add a little more oil.

This way of roasting peppers is a wardrobe basic—mix in some olives or slivers of anchovy and throw over some chopped parsley or egg. The layering gives the salad another dimension, with the practicality that you can assemble the whole caboodle well in advance of eating.

roasted pepper, arugula, and parmesan salad

4 red or orange peppers, core, seeds, and membranes removed

4–5 sprigs of fresh thyme

2 bay leaves

3 garlic cloves, peeled and sliced

6 tablespoons extra virgin olive oil

sea salt, black pepper

1 tablespoon balsamic vinegar

peanut oil for shallow frying

2 large slices of white bread, ½ inch thick, crusts removed, diced

3½ ounces thinly sliced Parmesan

a handful of arugula (preferably wild)

Serves 4

Preheat the oven to 400°F. Cut each pepper into 8 long strips and arrange in a crowded single layer in a roasting dish. Mix in the herbs and scatter over the garlic. Drizzle over 2 tablespoons of the olive oil and season. Roast for 45–50 minutes, stirring and basting at least twice to ensure the peppers emerge succulent and evenly singed at the edges. When they come out of the oven, drip over the vinegar, vaguely stir to mix it into the juices, and pour over the remaining 4 tablespoons of olive oil. Leave to cool.

In the meantime, heat about ¼ inch of peanut oil in a large frying pan over medium heat until hot enough to immerse a cube of bread in bubbles. Add the bread cubes and fry, turning frequently, until evenly gold and crisp. Remove them using a slotted spoon and drain on a double thickness of paper towel. Leave to cool.

Transfer the peppers and juices to a large, deep salad bowl. Arrange the Parmesan on top, then the arugula, and finally scatter over the croutons. Cover with plastic wrap and set aside in a cool place. Just before eating, gently toss the salad ingredients together using two salad servers.

A lusciously thick honey sauce, the consistency of mayonnaise, that combined with feta and pine nuts whisks us off somewhere in the vicinity of Crete.

eggplants in honey

2 eggplants, stalk ends discarded,
   thickly sliced (about ½ inch)
extra virgin olive oil
sea salt, black pepper
⅓ cup pine nuts
1 teaspoon Dijon mustard
2 teaspoons honey (ideally dark)
4 tablespoons peanut or
   vegetable oil
a squeeze of lemon juice
5 ounces feta, crumbled
seeds of ½ pomegranate
a handful of small fresh mint leaves

Serves 6

Heat a large non-stick frying pan over medium heat (or you could use two). Take as many eggplant slices as will fit into the pan, brush them on one side with olive oil, season, and fry this side for 4–6 minutes, until golden. Brush the top side with oil, turn the slices over and fry this side for 3–4 minutes. Transfer the slices to a large plate and cook the remainder likewise. Leave the eggplant to cool.

At the same time, preheat the oven to 400°F, spread the pine nuts out in a thin layer in a small baking dish and toast them for 8–10 minutes until lightly golden.

To prepare the sauce, whisk the mustard and honey together in a small bowl, and gradually whisk in the peanut oil until you have a thick emulsion. Whisk in a squeeze of lemon juice until the sauce has a thick trickling consistency. You can prepare the recipe to this point in advance.

Arrange the eggplants either on a couple of large plates for handing around, or on 6 individual ones. Drizzle the sauce over the eggplants, scatter over the feta, pomegranate seeds, pine nuts, and mint, and serve.

What could be nicer than breadcrumbs infused with garlic and anchovies stuffed inside red peppers? These are great as part of a Mediterranean mixed spread, and have a real hot-weather vibe to them, by which you can read relaxed.

anchovy-stuffed peppers

4 red or yellow peppers, or a mixture

sea salt, black pepper

extra virgin olive oil

5 garlic cloves, peeled and finely chopped

2 tablespoons fresh thyme leaves

15 salted anchovies, chopped

a knife tip of finely chopped dried chile

3 cups fresh white breadcrumbs

Serves 4

Preheat the oven to 400°F. Halve the peppers, keeping the stalks intact, and remove the seeds and membranes. Arrange the peppers cut side up in a roasting tray and season them inside with salt and pepper.

Heat a couple of tablespoons of olive oil in a large frying pan over medium heat, add the garlic, and briefly fry until aromatic and starting to color. Stir in the thyme, anchovies, and chile, then the breadcrumbs. Remove from the heat and mix in another 5 tablespoons of olive oil. Use the mixture to loosely stuff the peppers, then drizzle a little more olive oil on top, and roast for 40–45 minutes, until the crumbs are golden and crisp. Leave to cool to room temperature.

The best sun-dried tomatoes are only semi-dry, and have the succulence of fresh tomatoes with the intensity of dried. These slow-roasted, candy-sweet tomato petals are exquisite eaten with a tart goat cheese and thick slices of toasted French bread drizzled with olive oil.

slow-roasted tomatoes

3 pounds medium tomatoes
4 unpeeled garlic cloves, crushed
5 sprigs of fresh thyme
sea salt
superfine sugar
extra virgin olive oil
a handful of fresh basil leaves

Serves 8

Preheat the oven to 275°F. Bring a large pan of water to a boil. Cut out a cone from the top of each tomato to remove the core and plunge them first into the boiling water for 20 seconds and then into cold water. Remove them and slip off the skins, then halve and de-seed them. Lay the tomato halves cut side down on a non-stick baking tray, scatter over the garlic and thyme, and season with salt and a sprinkling of sugar. Drizzle over 4 tablespoons of olive oil and bake for 2 hours.

Once they are cool, place the tomatoes in a bowl or jar interspersed with the basil leaves, and cover with olive oil. If not serving immediately, cover and chill for up to three days, bringing back to room temperature before serving.

This famous Turkish dish is so-called because the Imam fainted with pleasure either from eating it or at the shock at the amount of oil used to cook it. Traditionally the eggplants are braised, while here they are roasted. You could also throw some pitted black olives over the eggplants when you serve them.

imam bayildi

2 eggplants
extra virgin olive oil
sea salt, black pepper
2 beefsteak tomatoes
  (approx. ½ pound each)
1 large onion, peeled, halved,
  and sliced
5 garlic cloves, peeled
  and finely chopped
3 tablespoons each coarsely chopped
  fresh flat-leaf parsley, dill, and basil

Serves 4

Preheat the oven to 400°F and heat a ridged grill pan over medium heat for several minutes. Trim the stalk ends of the eggplants and halve them lengthways. Brush them all over with oil and season. Grill the cut surface for about 5 minutes until golden, then lay the eggplant halves cut side up in a baking dish. You will probably need to grill them in two batches.

In the meantime, bring a small pan of water to a boil and cut out a cone to remove the core from each tomato. Plunge them into the boiling water for about 20 seconds and then into cold water. Slip off their skins and coarsely chop them. Combine them in a bowl with the onion, garlic, and herbs, add some seasoning and 6 tablespoons of olive oil, and toss.

Pile the vegetable mixture on top of the eggplants and roast for 40–45 minutes, until the vegetables are nicely golden. Leave to cool for at least 15 minutes, and serve either warm or at room temperature, with more olive oil poured on top.

Zucchini changes character completely when it is grilled—it's hard to believe it is the same vegetable as when eaten raw. This very simple means of cooking zucchini strips on a ridged grill pan brings out their sweet aromatic succulence with the minimum of fuss.

grilled zucchini with pine nuts

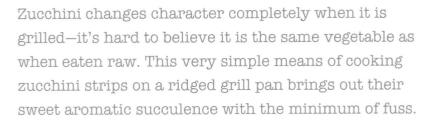

½ cup pine nuts
4 medium zucchini, trimmed and
   sliced lengthways into strips
   ¼ inch thick
extra virgin olive oil
sea salt, black pepper

Serves 6

Heat a dry frying pan over medium heat and toast the pine nuts, stirring constantly until they are golden and fragrant.

Heat a ridged grill pan over medium heat. Lay some of the zucchini slices out on a cutting board, brush one side with olive oil, season, and grill oiled side down until striped. Brush the top side with oil (but don't season it), then turn and cook this side too. Repeat with the remaining zucchini slices, moving them to a container as they are cooked. Splash over some olive oil, cover, and leave in a cool place. Stir in the pine nuts shortly before serving.

gratins

Gratins are the yummy factor in all things vegetable, big comforting pies with crusty edges concealing meltingly tender vegetables within. They are the antithesis of lightly steamed vegetables with a dab of butter, there is no holding back on the olive oil or cream, and most are a play on our love of grilled cheese.

Little spreads comfort like the silken elasticity of a warm cover of mozzarella or a bubbling mass of Cheddar. The likes of Gorgonzola and Roquefort melt down to a salty river. Goat cheeses in the mold of Crottins de Chavignol are rendered mousse-like and fluffy, while the mountain greats like Gruyère, Emmental, and Raclette lead the way to fonduesque nirvana.

The most austere of vegetables invite us into a nostalgic comfort zone when cooked as gratins. The silken texture of vegetables such as spinach fuse seamlessly with molten cheese, while the normally dour sprout is reborn as a vamp when roasted with Dolcelatte. Slices of ripe tomato baked with lily-white goat cheese exude a gorgeous pool of juices at the ready for a pile of toast.

Potatoes, however, are in a league of their own, in fact no need for cheese at all with that prized crispy top layer to divide up. And if you are looking for something lighter, then the potato gratins tick all the alluring boxes without being unduly rich. Tossed with just a little olive oil, you can dig into them with a big green salad and together they make a pretty virtuous lineup. The root vegetable and Cheddar gratin too is deceptively healthy, tasting a great deal more indulgent than it really is.

Soft coils of molten mozzarella straight from the oven with an inky dark green mass of spinach is heartstopping good. But like any other fonduesque dish it does require diners to be at the ready the moment it emerges, to capture it at its best. A lightly poached egg would also be divine here, veering in the direction of eggs Florentine.

spinach and mozzarella gratin

extra virgin olive oil

2 red onions, peeled, halved,
  and finely sliced

2 garlic cloves, peeled and
  finely chopped

sea salt, black pepper

2½ pounds spinach

12 ounces buffalo mozzarella (drained
  weight), sliced

½ pound baby plum tomatoes, halved

3 tablespoons oregano or
  marjoram leaves

thick slices of olive or sourdough
  bread, toasted and drizzled with
  olive oil, to serve

Serves 6

Heat a couple of tablespoons of oil in a large frying pan over medium heat. Add the onions and fry for 8–10 minutes, stirring frequently, until silky and golden, adding the garlic and some seasoning just before the end, then transfer them to a bowl. You will need to cook the spinach in batches. Heat another tablespoon of oil in the frying pan, add a large pile of spinach, and fry, tossing constantly until it wilts. Transfer it to a bowl and cook the remainder in the same fashion. Leave to cool.

Preheat the oven to 400°F. Transfer the spinach to a colander and press out the excess water using a potato masher. Lay half the leaves over the base of a 12-inch oval gratin dish or one of equivalent size, season, then lay over half the onions and half the mozzarella and repeat. Scatter the tomatoes and oregano on top. (You can prepare the gratin to this point in advance, in which case cover and chill.) Season, drizzle over another couple of tablespoons of oil, and bake for 25–30 minutes, until the cheese is golden and sizzling. Serve immediately, with thick slices of toast drizzled with olive oil.

Brussels sprouts and cabbages are never so good as when they turn golden and crispy at the tips. With drizzles of blue cheese, this would be yummy served with a seared steak or roast beef, though dedicated vegophiles will be happy to dive in there on its own and call it supper.

gratin of vegetables

1½ Sweetheart or pointed cabbages, base trimmed, outer leaves discarded

1 pound Brussels sprouts, base trimmed, outer leaves discarded, and halved downwards

1 red onion, peeled, halved, and thinly sliced

3 tablespoons extra virgin olive oil

sea salt, black pepper

7 ounces Dolcelatte, diced

Serves 4

Bring a large pan of salted water to a boil. Cut the Sweetheart cabbage into thin wedges, leaving them attached by the thick central stalk at the base. Add the cabbage and sprouts to the pan and bring back to a boil. Cook for 3 minutes, then drain into a colander and shake dry.

Preheat the oven to 425°F. Arrange the cabbage and sprouts with the red onion in a large roasting dish (e.g. 10 x 15 inch), drizzle over the olive oil, lightly season, and roast for 25 minutes, stirring halfway through. Mix in the diced cheese, return the dish to the oven for another few minutes, and serve immediately.

A lovely succulent gratin, in fact the only dry land in sight is the crispy breadcrumb layer on top, and even then there's still plenty of call for a baguette to mop up all the sweet oily juices.

gratin of tomatoes and goat cheese

extra virgin olive oil

1 red onion, peeled, halved,
    and thinly sliced

2½ pounds tomatoes

4 Crottins de Chavignol (2 ounces
    each), or other semi-matured
    goat cheese

sea salt, black pepper

1 tablespoon fresh thyme leaves

2 garlic cloves, peeled
    and finely chopped

⅔ cup fresh white or
    sourdough breadcrumbs

Serves 6

Preheat a tablespoon of oil in a large frying pan over medium heat. Add the onion and cook for 6–7 minutes until golden, stirring occasionally, then transfer it to a bowl. Bring a large pan of water to a boil. Cut out a cone from the top of each tomato, dunk them into the boiling water for about 20 seconds, and then into cold water. Slip off the skins and thinly slice them. Likewise thinly slice the Crottins into rounds, discarding the end rinds—you should get four or five slices from each one.

Assemble the gratin in a 12-inch gratin dish or other shallow ovenproof dish of a similar size. Arrange half the tomatoes and goat cheese in overlapping slices in rows, so you have a couple of slices of tomato to each one of goat cheese (reserve the ends of tomato until last, as you probably won't need them, and they can be saved for some other use). Season and scatter over half the thyme and garlic, then trickle over a tablespoon of oil. Repeat this layer.

Scatter the onion over the top, then toss the breadcrumbs with a tablespoon of oil, and scatter on top. You can prepare the gratin to this point up to about an hour in advance.

Heat the oven to 400°F, and bake the gratin for 35–40 minutes, until golden and crisp. Let it stand for 10 minutes before serving.

Despite its Provençal credentials, the combination of eggplant and tomatoes cannot but fail to transport us to a Mamma Mia-perfect craggy Greek coastline. Either way we're beside the Mediterranean, toasting the setting sun with a rough white wine, and that leads to thoughts of crispy red mullet or sardines hot from the grill, or some barbecued lamb.

provençal gratin

2 medium eggplants
extra virgin olive oil
sea salt, black pepper
1½ pounds potatoes, peeled
3 garlic cloves, peeled and
    crushed to a paste
2 beefsteak tomatoes
    (1½ pounds)
1 red onion, peeled, halved,
    and thinly sliced
1⅓ cups fresh white
    breadcrumbs
3 tablespoons fresh marjoram
    or oregano leaves

Serves 4–6

Preheat the oven to 400°F. Cut the eggplants across into slices ½ inch thick, discarding the ends. Heat a large frying pan, or even better two. Brush one side of each slice of eggplant with oil, season, and fry this side until golden. Brush the top side with oil, turn, and fry this side too. As the slices are cooked, arrange them in overlapping rows in a 12 x 8-inch gratin dish (ideally cast iron).

Slice the potatoes as thinly as possible—a food processor fitted with a fine slicing attachment makes light work of this. Toss them in a bowl with 2 tablespoons of olive oil, the garlic, and some seasoning. Lay them, overlapping, on top of the eggplant. Don't worry too much about looks here as they'll be concealed by the next layer—as long as they lie evenly that's fine. Press down with your hands. Cover tightly with foil and bake for about 45 minutes, until the potatoes are tender when pierced with a knife.

In the meantime, bring a pan of water to a boil. Cut out a cone from the top of each tomato to remove the core and plunge them into the water for about 20 seconds, then into cold water. Slip off their skins and slice them across, discarding the bottom slices or keeping them for some other use. Lay the sliced tomatoes in overlapping rows on top of the potato and season. Scatter over the onion and drizzle over 2 tablespoons of oil. Toss the breadcrumbs with another couple of tablespoons of oil and scatter these over, then the marjoram or oregano. Give everything a final drizzle of oil. Turn the oven up to 425°F and pop the gratin back in for another 20–25 minutes, until golden. The gratin can be successfully reheated for 20–25 minutes in a medium oven.

Just the one layer of butternut squash here that cooks to a gorgeously melting consistency between two layers of potatoes. For life beyond Swiss Gruyère, look to their French equivalents Beaufort, Comte, and Abondance, also Swiss Appenzeller, all are strong cheeses that succeed in being delicate and elegant at the same time.

gratin of butternut squash, potato, and gruyère

2 x 1½ pound butternut squashes

1¾ pounds potatoes

4 tablespoons extra virgin olive oil

3 garlic cloves, peeled and crushed
  to a paste

sea salt, black pepper

a handful of fresh sage leaves

4 tablespoons heavy cream

1⅓ cups grated Gruyère

Serves 6

Preheat the oven to 400°F. Cut the skin off the squashes, then cut off the trunks and thinly slice into rounds. Halve the bulb, cut out the seeds and thinly slice into crescents.

Peel and slice the potatoes as thinly as possible, discarding the ends—you can use the slicing attachment on a food processor for this. Toss them in a large bowl with half each of the olive oil and garlic, and some seasoning. Toss the squash with the remaining olive oil, garlic, and some seasoning in another large bowl. Lay half the potatoes in rows of overlapping slices in a 8 x 12-inch gratin dish or shallow ovenproof dish of a similar size. Lay the squash on top, first arranging the round pieces in rows of overlapping slices, then fitting the crescents on top as neatly as possible. Top with a final layer of potatoes. Press down with your hands, but don't worry if it seems a little bulky, it will sink as it cooks. Cover tightly with foil and bake for 50 minutes, until the gratin is tender when pierced with a knife.

Turn the oven up to 425°F. Lay the sage leaves on top of the gratin, drizzle over the cream, and scatter over the cheese. Return the gratin to the oven for 15–25 minutes, until the cheese is golden and bubbling. It can also be cooked in advance and reheated in an oven preheated to 425°F for 20 minutes.

As good eaten cold as hot, when all the punchy Mediterranean flavors shine through. Try to buy a really good pesto from a deli if not making your own, then you can pick up the necessary loaf of bread while you're there.

roasted pepper, goat cheese, and pesto gratin

8 red peppers

4 tomatoes

3 tablespoons extra virgin olive oil

sea salt, black pepper

7 ounces goat cheese, rind removed, thinly sliced

4 tablespoons pesto

Serves 4–6

Preheat the oven to 400°F, and roast the peppers on an oven rack for 20 minutes. Place them inside a plastic bag (you may like to put this inside another plastic bag to make sure it doesn't leak), wrap up the bag and set aside for several hours or overnight to cool.

Skin the peppers, discarding the core and seeds. If necessary give them a quick rinse under cold water, then cut them into wide strips. Bring a small pan of water to a boil and cut out a cone from the top of each tomato to remove the core. Plunge them into the boiling water for about 20 seconds and then into cold water. Slip off the skins and slice them.

Heat the oven to 425°F. Drizzle 1 tablespoon of oil over the base of a 12-inch oval gratin dish or other shallow ovenproof dish of a similar size. Arrange half the peppers over the base and season them. Lay half the goat cheese over, then the sliced tomatoes, and spoon over half the pesto. Lay the remaining peppers in place, season them, and scatter over the remaining goat cheese. Dollop over the rest of the pesto and another couple of tablespoons of olive oil and bake for 25–30 minutes. Serve warm rather than piping hot, about 30 minutes out of the oven, or at room temperature.

Anything that's finely sliced and cooked to within a whisker of collapse enters the comfort zone. But this is pretty healthy to boot, deceptively creamy, though in essence a mass of tender wintery roots with a little melted cheese and some crisp breadcrumbs.

root vegetable and cheddar gratin

1 pound carrots, trimmed, peeled,
   and thinly sliced
1 pound parsnips, trimmed, peeled,
   and thinly sliced
1 pound leeks (trimmed weight), thinly sliced
1 cup vegetable stock
2 tablespoons unsalted butter, diced
sea salt, black pepper
1½ teaspoons superfine sugar
4 medium eggs
¾ cup grated mature Cheddar
¾ cup fresh white breadcrumbs
2 tablespoons peanut
   or vegetable oil
6 tablespoons coarsely chopped
   fresh flat-leaf parsley

Serves 6

Place the carrots, parsnips, and leeks in a large saucepan with the stock, butter, 1½ teaspoons of salt, and the sugar and bring the liquid to a boil. Cover the pan and cook over medium heat for 5 minutes, then cook uncovered for another 15 minutes, stirring occasionally, until nearly all the liquid has evaporated and the vegetables are sitting in a buttery emulsion. Leave to cool for a few minutes.

Whisk the eggs in a large bowl with some seasoning, then stir in two-thirds of the cheese. Toss the breadcrumbs in another bowl with the oil, then mix in the rest of the cheese. Add the vegetables to the bowl with the egg and cheese mixture, scatter the parsley over, and stir to combine everything. Tip the mixture into a 12-inch oval gratin dish or other shallow ovenproof dish of a similar size. Smooth the surface and scatter the breadcrumb mixture on top. The gratin can be made up to this point several hours in advance, in which case scatter the breadcrumbs over at the last minute, cover, and chill.

Preheat the oven to 425°F. Place the gratin dish in a roasting dish with boiling water coming two-thirds of the way up the sides, and bake for 30–35 minutes, until the breadcrumbs are golden and crusty. Serve immediately.

This is a celebration of all the young vegetables that appear in the spring—lightly cooked and coated in a creamy béchamel sauce and lots of cheese.

gratin of spring vegetables

1½ pounds young or baby turnips,
   romanesco broccoli florets,
   carrots, and zucchini, trimmed
   and peeled if necessary
⅔ cup white wine
3½ tablespoons unsalted butter
⅓ cup all-purpose flour
1⅓ cup milk
¾ cup heavy cream
1 bay leaf
sea salt, black pepper
6½ ounces Gruyère, sliced

Serves 6

Preheat the oven to 400°F. Bring a large pan of salted water to a boil. Depending on the size of the turnips, quarter or cut them into wedges, and do the same with the baby broccoli. Add the turnips and carrots to the pan and cook for about 7 minutes, adding the zucchini and broccoli quarters 3 minutes before the end. Drain them into a colander and leave for a few minutes for the surface water to evaporate.

In the meantime, make the sauce. Pour the wine into a small non-stick saucepan and reduce to a third of its volume, then transfer it to a bowl. Melt the butter in the same pan, add the flour, and cook the roux for 1–2 minutes. Gradually incorporate the milk, cream, and reduced wine off the heat, whisking to disperse any lumps, then add the bay leaf. Return to the heat and simmer for 5 minutes, stirring occasionally, then season with salt and pepper.

Arrange the vegetables with the sauce and the cheese in a 12-inch oval gratin dish or other shallow ovenproof dish of an equivalent size, discarding the bay leaf. Bake for 30–35 minutes, until golden and bubbling at the edges. Spoon off any buttery fat on the surface before serving.

Crusty top and bottom and fluffy mashed potatoes in between, set with teasing little pockets of salty Cheddar. I always get huge pleasure out of marrying these mashed potatoes with roast chicken, or a shoulder of lamb studded with garlic and rosemary. When so often the great Swiss cheeses get the upper hand, it's satisfying to sit down to something more British.

cheese and potato soufflé

Mashed Potatoes

2 pounds potatoes, peeled and cut
    into even chunks

3½ tablespoons salted butter, diced,
    plus extra for greasing

6 tablespoons freshly grated Parmesan

1 cup whole milk

sea salt, black pepper

freshly grated nutmeg

3 medium egg whites

7 ounces mature Cheddar, cut into
    ½ inch dice

Herb Salad

1 small handful of arugula leaves
    (ideally wild)

3 tablespoons each of small fresh
    flat-leaf parsley and mint leaves

3 scallions, trimmed and cut into
    fine strips about 2 inches long

4–6 tablespoons extra virgin olive oil

1 teaspoon lemon juice

sea salt

Bring a large pan of salted water to a boil, add the potatoes, and simmer until tender.

Preheat the oven to 425°F. Generously butter a 12-inch oval gratin dish or other ovenproof dish of a similar size and dust it with a couple of tablespoons of grated Parmesan.

Drain the potatoes into a colander, then pass through a food mill or sieve into a large bowl. Add the butter, and once this has melted stir in the milk, some seasoning, and a grating of nutmeg. You should have a sloppy mash. Whisk the egg whites in a medium bowl until stiff, using an electric whisk, and fold these into the mash in two turns, followed by the diced cheese. Taste to check the seasoning. Transfer the mixture into the prepared dish, scatter the rest of the Parmesan over, and bake for 20–25 minutes, until puffy and golden. Serve immediately with the herb salad below—you want to capture all those little cheese pockets while they're gooey.

To make the herb salad, toss the arugula and herbs in a bowl and mix in the scallions. Serve a pile of this on top of each serving of potato, and drizzle over a tablespoon of olive oil, squeeze over a little lemon, and scatter over a few flakes of sea salt.

Pasta gratins begin and end with macaroni and cheese, with everything in between being a homage. Here rigatoni—the four by four of macaroni—takes center stage, and lip-service is paid to a few veggies by way of fried eggplant and a tomato sauce. But it's still macaroni and cheese.

gratin of rigatoni with eggplant and mozzarella

Béchamel

3½ tablespoons unsalted butter
½ cup flour
2 cups whole milk
sea salt, black pepper
1 bay leaf
1⅓ cups freshly grated Parmesan

Gratin

extra virgin olive oil
2 eggplants, sliced ½ inch thick
½ pound rigatoni
2 buffalo mozzarellas, drained
  and sliced
½ cup breadcrumbs

Tomato Sauce

1 dried red chile, finely chopped
4 garlic cloves, peeled and chopped
6 tablespoons chopped fresh
  flat-leaf parsley
10 ounces passata or tomatoes, cooked,
  peeled, chopped, and sieved

To make the béchamel, melt the butter in a small non-stick saucepan over medium heat, stir in the flour, and allow the roux to seethe for about a minute. Working off the heat, gradually incorporate the milk using a wooden spoon, a little at a time to begin with. Season the sauce, add the bay leaf, bring to a boil stirring frequently, and simmer for 10 minutes, giving it a stir every now and then. If it seems lumpy at the end, give it a quick whisk. Discard the bay leaf and stir in the Parmesan.

Heat a large frying pan over medium heat. You will need to cook the eggplant slices in batches. Brush one side with olive oil, season, and fry oiled side down until golden. Brush the top side with oil, turn, and fry until golden too. Remove and repeat with the remaining eggplant slices.

At the same time, bring a large pot of salted water to a boil. Add the pasta and give it a stir. Cook until almost tender, on the firm side of al dente, then drain into a colander, and briefly run under cold water. Return it to the pot and toss with a tablespoon of olive oil.

To make the tomato sauce, heat 1 tablespoon of oil in a clean frying pan over medium heat, add the chile and garlic, and as soon as it starts to color add the parsley and stir to coat it in oil. Pour in the passata and season. Bring to a boil and simmer for a couple of minutes.

Preheat the oven to 400°F. To assemble the gratin, coat the base of an 8 x 12-inch roasting dish with a couple of tablespoons of the tomato sauce. Layer half the pasta on top, then half each of the tomato sauce, eggplant slices, and mozzarella. Repeat with the remaining half of the ingredients.

Give the béchamel a quick whisk and smooth it over the surface. Toss the breadcrumbs with a tablespoon of oil and some seasoning and scatter on top.* Bake the gratin for 35 minutes, until the surface is golden and bubbling.

* This gratin can be prepared to this point in advance, in which case cover it with plastic wrap, leave it to cool completely, and then chill. It may need a little longer in the oven.

main courses

This chapter could be seen as an impostor, given that so many of the dishes in this book will stand in as a main course. Most of us will be quite happy with a gratin or a gorgeous big salad for supper with no further ado. But every now and again, especially if you've got someone coming around to lunch or supper and want a veggie "main" course that is very obviously a main course and has that finger-clicking demand for attendant salads, then a lovely tart, a pie, or a big omelette has a certain presence.

I've always derived enormous satisfaction from making tarts—while bread-making is altogether forbidding to the techno-shy, these boost your confidence in inverse proportion to your skill. Anyone can make pastry. But before we get to that point, we have the joys of ready-made puff, which makes for the simplest of pizza-style miniature tarts for eating by hand. And it extends its talents to large oblong tarts, such as the one laid out with neat rows of asparagus spears. But the real spectacular is the mushroom Pithivier with its scalloped edges, which belongs somewhere in a salon with all things Louis XIV.

Returning to hands-on skill, you will actually get better results making pastry in a food processor than by hand. This leads on to classic quiche-type tarts such as spinach and Gruyère, so commonplace it is all too easy to forget just how good it can be. With such tarts it's a case of how you serve them and not when you serve them; they're fab at any time, brunch onwards.

The same compliments can be paid to frittata, a winning Italian way with eggs that bypasses the usual sleight of hand called for in flipping or rolling them out of the pan. They are cooked first on the stove in a frying pan and then under the broiler until they are puffy and golden. Like tortes, which are something like a quiche without the pastry layered into a cake tin, they spill their largesse from messy puffed edges. Both emerge impressively golden and crusty.

These little pizzettas tend to be preyed upon by wandering fingers long before they are cool, but they can be eaten cold, and are great for picnics or cut into bite-size quarters with a preprandial drink.

cherry tomato pizzettas

10 ounces puff pastry (1 pre-rolled
   sheet)
Dijon mustard
11 ounces cherry tomatoes, halved
1 egg yolk, blended with
   1 tablespoon water
sea salt, black pepper
1 ounce finely shaved Parmesan
extra virgin olive oil

Serves 6

Preheat the oven to 425°F. Thinly roll out the pastry on a lightly floured work surface, half at a time if it's easier, and cut out 2½ x 5-inch circles using a bowl or plate as a guide. Arrange these on a couple of baking trays.

Spread a little Dijon mustard in the center of each circle, to within about 1 inch of the rim. Place the tomatoes on top. Brush the surrounding rim with the egg wash, then season the tomatoes, cover with a few shavings of Parmesan, drizzle a little olive oil on top, and bake for 15–20 minutes, until golden and risen. Serve hot or cold.

Cut into wedges these make lovely appetizers, as well as serving as a light lunch or a prelude to a heavier one. They are at their prettiest made with red chicory.

chicory, prune, and blue cheese pizzettas

18 ounces puff pastry

4 ounces Fourme d'Ambert or other blue cheese, diced

4 ounces stoned prunes (about ½ cup), sliced

2–3 heads of red or white chicory (depending on size), base trimmed and outer leaves discarded

2 tablespoons extra virgin olive oil

sea salt, black pepper

1 egg yolk, blended with 1 tablespoon water

coarsely chopped fresh flat-leaf parsley to serve

Serves 6

Thinly roll out the pastry on a lightly floured work surface, half at a time if it's easier, and cut out 2½ x 5-inch circles using a bowl or plate as a guide. Combine the cheese and prunes in a large bowl.

To finish making the tarts, preheat the oven to 425°F. Arrange the pastry bases on two large baking sheets. Halve the chicory heads, cut them into long thin strips, and halve again if longer than about 3 inches. Toss these with the cheese and prunes, the olive oil, and some seasoning. Pile the mixture into the center of the tarts, leaving a 1 inch rim. Brush this with the egg wash and bake for 15–20 minutes, until the pastry rim is golden and risen and the filling has begun to color. Scatter some parsley on top, and serve immediately, or warm about 20 minutes later. They can also be reheated. In this case save scattering the parsley on top until the last minute.

Leeks, like onions, roast beautifully. A spell in the oven concentrates their sweetness, making salty feta a perfect partner.

leek and feta pizzettas

2 tablespoons unsalted butter
2 tablespoons extra virgin olive oil
3 leeks, trimmed and thinly sliced
sea salt, black pepper
1 tablespoon fresh lemon thyme leaves
10 ounces puff pastry (1 pre-rolled
   sheet)
5 ounces feta, crumbled or diced
coarsely chopped fresh flat-leaf
   parsley to serve

Serves 6

Preheat the oven to 425°F. Melt the butter in a large frying pan over medium heat with half the olive oil, and once the froth subsides add the leeks. Season and fry for a few minutes until softened, without coloring, then stir in the thyme.

Thinly roll out the pastry on a lightly floured work surface, half at a time if it's easier, and cut out 2½ x 5-inch circles using a bowl or plate as a guide. Arrange these on a couple of baking trays.

Gently fold the cheese into the leeks. Scatter this over the pastry circles to within ½ inch of the rim, drizzle with 1 tablespoon of oil, and bake for 15 minutes. Serve hot or at room temperature, scattered with parsley. They can also be reheated.

Homage to those big pans of filo tart with spinach and feta that grace the rickety tables of seaside Greek tavernas beneath scanty bamboo mats for shade.

summer leaf filo pie

1 pound young spinach leaves

2 tablespoons extra virgin olive oil

4 leeks, trimmed and sliced

1 tablespoon fresh thyme leaves

sea salt, black pepper

7 tablespoons unsalted butter, melted,
   plus 2 tablespoons

4 garlic cloves, peeled
   and finely chopped

⅔ cup fresh flat-leaf parsley,
   coarsely chopped

⅔ cup watercress, coarsely chopped

10 ounces feta, cut into ½ inch dice

1 x 16-ounce package of filo pastry

Serves 6

Bring a large pan of salted water to a boil. Add half the spinach and blanch it for 2 minutes, then transfer it to a colander in the sink using a slotted spatula, and repeat with the remainder. Using a potato masher, press out as much of the water as possible—it's important to remove all the excess so that the pastry doesn't go soggy when it's cooked.

At the same time, heat the olive oil in a large frying pan over medium heat. Add the leeks, thyme, and some seasoning and fry them for 5–10 minutes until soft and lightly colored, stirring now and then. Transfer them to a large bowl.

Melt the 2 tablespoons of butter in the pan you cooked the leeks in over medium heat. Add the garlic and briefly fry until aromatic, then add the spinach, season, and cook for a few minutes to infuse it with the garlic, stirring occasionally. Add to the bowl with the leeks and leave to cool.

To cook the pie, preheat the oven to 400°F. To finish preparing the filling, mix the chopped parsley, watercress, and feta into the cooked vegetables. Lay the pile of filo pastry out on the work surface and select an 8 x 12-inch baking dish. Using this as a guide, trim the pile of pastry, using a sharp knife, so it is ½ inch larger than the top of the dish, allowing for shrinkage.

Paint the bottom of the dish with melted butter, then paint the top sheet of pastry, lay it in place, and repeat until you have about seven sheets layered—they will come a little of the way up the sides of the dish. Spoon the filling evenly over the pastry, and layer with another seven sheets of pastry, again painting each one with butter before laying it in place. Using a sharp knife, score the top sheet into six squares and bake the pie for 40 minutes. Serve immediately, while the pastry is crisp.

Made as a big slab on a baking tray, this plays on the graphic beauty of asparagus to form neat lines and rectangles, so contrary to most food. That said it's messier to eat than it looks, and it's paper napkins all around.

asparagus tray tart

1 pound finger-thick asparagus spears
10 ounces puff pastry (1 pre-rolled sheet)
2 medium egg yolks
⅔ cup sour cream
½ teaspoon Dijon mustard
2 tablespoons freshly grated Parmesan
sea salt, black pepper

Serves 4

Preheat the oven to 400°F. Bring a large pan of salted water to a boil. Trim the asparagus spears where they begin to become woody and peel to within 1 inch of the tip. Add to the pan, bring back to a boil, and cook for 4 minutes. Drain and refresh in cold water. Remove and dry on a kitchen towel.

Roll the pastry into a rectangle 16 x 8 inches and trim to neaten the edges—make sure you have a baking sheet large enough, otherwise adjust the dimensions accordingly. Lay the pastry on the baking sheet, and lay the asparagus in rows of single spears, so there is a pastry surround of 1 inch. Beat the egg yolks and paint the pastry border. Bake the tart for 15 minutes.

Blend the sour cream, mustard, Parmesan, remaining beaten egg yolks, and seasoning together in a bowl. Spoon this over the asparagus and bake for another 15 minutes until golden on the top. Serve 5 minutes out of the oven, although it is also excellent cold.

Bubble and squeak is one of very few home-grown peasant dishes that remain a part of the English repertoire. And yet for a rustic dish it's surprisingly difficult to get right, or at least as good as I recall from my childhood. This pie has all the comfort: cabbage with potato is a wonderfully soothing marriage of humble leaf and spud. Your cabbage should be dark in hue with a lively bitterness—anything blond will be too tame.

bubble and squeak pie

1½ pounds new or red
  potatoes, peeled
4 ounces cabbage or leafy greens
  (trimmed weight)
2 tablespoons salted butter
1 onion, peeled and chopped
sea salt, white pepper
18 ounces puff pastry
7 ounces Lancashire or other
  cow's milk cheese, crumbled
1 egg yolk blended with
  1 tablespoon water

Serves 6

Bring two large pots of salted water to a boil. Add the potatoes to one and simmer until tender, then drain them into a colander, and leave for a few minutes to steam dry. Add the cabbage to the other pot, simmer for 3 minutes, then drain and leave to cool.

Melt the butter in a large frying pan over medium heat. Add the onion and fry for several minutes until softened, stirring occasionally, and without coloring. Coarsely mash the potatoes using a fork or a potato masher, then mix in the onion and the butter it cooked in, season with a little salt and white pepper, and leave to cool.

Preheat the oven to 400°F. Roll out two-thirds of the pastry on a lightly floured work surface to fit the inside of a 9-inch tart pan, 2 inches deep with a removable base, so it is large enough to drape over the sides. Lay it in place and trim the top. Fold the cheese into the potato and onion mixture. Scatter half of this over the base of the tart, gently press the mixture down, lay the cabbage leaves in a layer on top, lightly season, then scatter the rest of the potato on top.

Roll out the remaining pastry to fit the top (you can use the pan as a guide) and lay it over the potato. Brush the surface with the egg wash, then fold the rim down to seal the pie, and brush this edge with egg wash too. Cut four slits in the surface in the shape of a cross, to within an inch of the center. You can make the pie several hours in advance, in which case chill it. Bake for 40 minutes and serve hot or warm.

Pithiviers are splendid pies to behold, with their glazed domes and scalloped edges. The original of a sweet creamy frangipane sets the tone for other fillings, such as this rich wild mushroom purée. I would serve this with a salad of baby spinach dressed with extra virgin olive oil and balsamic vinegar, and with coarsely chopped toasted hazelnuts.

mushroom and herb pithivier

2 pounds mixed mushrooms (e.g. chestnut, portabello, shiitake), trimmed

4 tablespoons unsalted butter

4 shallots, peeled and finely chopped

sea salt, black pepper

4 ounces cream cheese

2 teaspoons finely chopped fresh tarragon

2 tablespoons snipped fresh chives

13 ounces puff pastry

1 egg yolk, blended with 1 tablespoon milk

Serves 6

Finely chop the mushrooms in a food processor, working in batches to avoid reducing them to complete mush. Melt the butter in two large frying pans over medium heat, and cook the mushrooms with the shallots and some seasoning for 12–15 minutes, stirring frequently, until the mixture is dry and pieces of mushroom begin to separate out. Transfer the mushroom purée to a bowl, cover, and leave it to cool, then blend in the cream cheese and herbs and taste for seasoning.

Thinly roll out half the pastry on a lightly floured work surface. Lay it on a baking sheet and, using an 8-inch cake pan or plate, mark a circle in the center. Smooth the mushroom purée inside the circle, using a palette knife to shape it into a disc. Roll out the remaining half of the pastry, brush the rim of the pie with the egg wash, and lay the sheet on top, smoothing it over the mushroom filling, and pressing the edges together. Now cut around the rim in a scalloped shape—it should look a little like a flower. You can prepare the pie to this point several hours in advance, in which case cover and chill it.

Preheat the oven to 400°F. Brush the top of the pie all over with the egg wash and then, using the tip of a sharp knife, trace lines on the top and the scallops at the side (traditionally these are curved). Bake the pie for 30 minutes and serve hot or warm. The pie can also be reheated.

An early summer tart with so many peas it leaves you in no doubt that good weather is on the way. Packs of fresh shelled peas are the greatest convenience since frozen, my one gripe being that we hardly ever see them in the pod any longer. It's such a pleasure popping open those smooth green pods and running your finger along the insides to extract the peas within, which are at their sweetest in the short time before you cook them.

pea, feta, and basil tart

2 tablespoons unsalted butter
½ teaspoon superfine sugar
sea salt, black pepper
1½ pounds fresh shelled peas
2 medium eggs, plus 1 yolk
1¼ cups heavy or whipping cream
¾ cup freshly grated Parmesan
5 ounces feta, cut into ½ inch dice
a handful of fresh basil leaves,
    torn into 2 or 3
1 x 9-inch tart case, 2 inches deep,
    pre-baked (see page 81)
1 tablespoon extra virgin olive oil

Serves 6

Preheat the oven to 400°F. Place ⅔ cup water in a large saucepan with the butter, sugar, and ½ teaspoon of salt. Bring to a boil over a high heat, add the peas, and cook for 5 minutes, stirring occasionally, until tender. Drain them into a sieve. Place half of them in a food processor and briefly break them up.

Whisk the eggs and yolk with the cream, some seasoning, and half the Parmesan in a large bowl. Fold in all the peas, half the feta, and the basil. Transfer the filling to the tart case and scatter the remaining feta and Parmesan on top. Drizzle the olive oil over the surface and bake the tart for 35–40 minutes, until golden and set in the center. Leave to cool for 20 minutes before serving. This tart is also good eaten at room temperature, and can be reheated.

The texture of this tart is positively exquisite, but its success lies in squeezing out every last drop of liquid from the cooked spinach to ensure it sets properly.

spinach and gruyère tart

1¾ pound spinach, washed

1¼ cups heavy or whipping cream

3 medium eggs

sea salt, black pepper

freshly grated nutmeg

1⅔ cups grated Gruyère

1 x 9-inch tart case, 2 inches deep,
    pre-baked (see opposite page)

4 ounces cherry tomatoes, halved

peanut oil

Serves 6

Preheat the oven to 400°F. You may need to cook the spinach in two pans, or in two batches. Place it in a large saucepan with just the water that clings to the leaves from washing, cover with a lid, and steam over medium heat for 10 minutes, stirring it halfway through, until it collapses. Drain it into a sieve, and press out as much liquid as possible using a potato masher. Either leave it to cool, or, using rubber gloves, squeeze balls of the spinach between your hands to extract every last trace of moisture, then slice it.

Whisk the cream, eggs, some seasoning, and a little grated nutmeg in a bowl. Stir in the spinach, making sure it is evenly distributed, and then half the Gruyère. Transfer this to the tart case and smooth the surface. Toss the cherry tomatoes in a bowl with just enough oil to coat them and a little seasoning. Scatter these over the surface of the tart and press them into the filling to level them with the spinach. Scatter the remaining cheese on top, mainly towards the center, and bake for 35–45 minutes, until golden on the surface and set. Leave to cool for 10–20 minutes before serving. While it is best eaten hot or warm from the oven, it does reheat successfully.

shortcrust pastry for a 9-inch tart case

2½ cups all-purpose flour

a pinch of sea salt

⅔ cup (about 10½ tablespoons)
   unsalted butter, chilled and diced

1 medium egg, separated

Place the flour and salt in the bowl of a food processor, add the butter, and reduce to a fine crumb-like consistency. Incorporate the egg yolk, and then with the motor running, trickle in just enough cold water for the dough to cling together into lumps. Transfer the pastry to a large bowl and bring it together into a ball, using your hands.

Wrap the pastry in plastic wrap and chill for at least 1 hour. It will keep well in the fridge for up to a couple of days.

Preheat the oven to 400°F. Knead the pastry until it is pliable. Thinly roll it out on a lightly floured surface and carefully lift it into a 9-inch tart pan with a removable base. This is quite a durable pastry and shouldn't tear or collapse. Press it into the corners of the tin and run a rolling pin over the top to trim the edges. Reserve the trimmings for patching the pastry case after it is baked. Prick the base with a fork and line it with a sheet of foil, tucking it over the top to secure the pastry sides to the pan. Now weight it with baking beans—dried pulses will do nicely.

Bake the pastry case for 15 minutes, then remove the foil and baking beans. If any of the sides have shrunk more than they should, use a little of the reserved pastry to patch them, bearing in mind that the tart can only be filled as far as the lowest point of the sides. Brush the base and sides of the case with the reserved egg white, then bake it for another 10 minutes until it is lightly colored. This glaze helps to seal the pastry and prevent the filling from soaking in.

tart pans

Given that pastry sometimes shrinks, it is a good idea to start off with a tart pan 2 inches deep. Failing that, you could forgo the crimped edges and use a cake pan with a removable collar—you can always trim the sides after cooking if they seem too deep. But I'd avoid china quiche dishes, which are rarely deep enough and make it difficult to serve the tart without damaging it.

These little omelettes with their lacy golden edges are delicious tucked inside a warm pocket of pita bread, or eaten with a green or tomato salad, as well as being ripe for nibbling by hand.

pea and parmesan fritters

Fritters

extra virgin olive oil

sea salt, black pepper

½ teaspoon superfine sugar

7 ounces fresh shelled peas

4 medium eggs

1 tablespoon lemon juice

½ cup freshly grated Parmesan

4 tablespoons coarsely chopped
   fresh flat-leaf parsley, plus extra
   to serve

Salad

arugula leaves

extra virgin olive oil

a squeeze of lemon juice

sea salt

a handful of Parmesan shavings

Serves 4

Place 2 tablespoons of olive oil in a medium saucepan with 3 tablespoons of water, ½ teaspoon of salt, and the sugar. Bring this to a simmer over high heat, then add the peas. Cook, tossing occasionally, for about 3 minutes until just tender, then drain.

Whisk the eggs in a large bowl with the lemon juice and some seasoning, and fold in the grated Parmesan, the peas, and parsley. You can do this a short time in advance.

Heat a large non-stick frying pan over high heat, add about 1 teaspoon of oil, and drop tablespoons of the mixture into the pan, spreading them out into omelettes 4 inches in diameter. Cook for about 1 minute each side, until really golden. You will need to do this in batches, draining them on a double thickness of paper towel as you go, and adding more oil to the pan as necessary.

Either transfer them to a serving plate and scatter a little more parsley on top, or serve piled with the salad below.

a little salad

Toss the arugula leaves with enough olive oil to coat them in a bowl, and season with a squeeze of lemon juice and a pinch of salt. Divide the fritters between four plates, pile the salad on top, sprinkle with Parmesan shavings, and drizzle with a little more oil.

Basil, Parmesan, and zucchini could charm the most jaded palate, and the baby zucchini has the edge here over anything larger.

zucchini frittata

¾ pound baby zucchini, ends trimmed, halved lengthways

3 tablespoons extra virgin olive oil

sea salt, black pepper

6 medium eggs

¼ cup freshly grated Parmesan

a large handful of fresh basil leaves, torn in half

1 ounce finely sliced Parmesan

Serves 4

Heat a ridged grill pan over medium heat for several minutes. Place the halved zucchini in a large bowl, drizzle with 2 tablespoons of olive oil, add some seasoning, and toss to coat them. If necessary, cook the zucchini in batches, turning them as they color on the underside, and cooking the second side. Move them to a plate—they don't have to be completely cool before the next stage, but equally they can be cooked in advance if wished.

Whisk the eggs in a bowl and stir in the grated Parmesan, basil leaves, and some seasoning. Fold in the grilled zucchini. Heat the broiler to high, and also heat a 10-inch frying pan with a heatproof handle over medium heat. Add a tablespoon of oil to the pan, add in the egg and zucchini mixture, and cook for 3 minutes. Scatter the Parmesan slices over the top of the omelette, drizzle with another tablespoon of oil, and place under the grill for 3–4 minutes, until golden and puffy on the sides. The frittata can be eaten hot or at room temperature.

This is for all those who feel Spanish omelettes are never quite deep enough. A springform cake pan ensures a luxury of layers you didn't even dream existed until you took your fork to it.

a very deep spanish omelette

4 tablespoons extra virgin olive oil

2 pounds new or red potatoes, peeled and thickly sliced

sea salt, black pepper

5 onions, peeled, halved and sliced

a knob of unsalted butter

¾ cup freshly grated Parmesan

3 medium eggs, plus 2 yolks

1¼ cup heavy cream

3 tablespoons coarsely chopped fresh flat-leaf parsley

Serves 6

Heat 2 tablespoons of olive oil in a large frying pan over medium heat. Add the potatoes and cook for about 5 minutes, turning them now and then to coat them in the oil. Season with salt, add ⅔ cup water to the pan, cover with a large lid, and cook over low heat for about 10 minutes, until the potatoes are just tender. Using the lid, drain off any excess water, and leave to cool, covered.

Heat another couple of tablespoons of oil in a large saucepan over medium heat. Add the onions and cook for 15–20 minutes, stirring frequently, until golden and silky. Season them, transfer to a bowl, and leave to cool.

Preheat the oven to 400°F. Use the butter to grease an 8-inch cake pan, 2 inches deep, with a removable base and dust it with a little grated Parmesan. Whisk the eggs and egg yolks, cream, parsley, half the remaining Parmesan, and some seasoning together in a bowl. Coat the base of the pan with a few tablespoons of this mixture, then use half the remainder to coat the potato slices, and mix the rest in with the onions. Lay half the potato slices over the base of the pan, spooning over half the egg, then the onions, then the rest of the potato slices, and egg mixture. Scatter the remaining Parmesan on top and bake for 45–50 minutes, until golden on the surface and set (you can check this by inserting a knife into the center—if it seems runny, give it a little longer, and if necessary you can cover the top with foil to stop it from coloring further). Run a knife around the collar of the omelette and leave it to cool to room temperature, when it will firm up. Serve it in wedges.

Wild mushrooms are principally to do with perfume—
if it is texture you are after, then flat-caps will serve
you just as well. So when you need a largish quantity
the best route is to take advantage of both. It doesn't
have to be any particular type of fungi, whatever's on
sale and the wallet allows.

wild mushroom torte

3½ tablespoons unsalted butter

1 cup freshly grated Parmesan

4 tablespoons extra virgin olive oil

2 shallots, peeled and finely chopped

1¾ pounds mixture of wild and
   cultivated mushrooms, trimmed
   and finely sliced

sea salt, black pepper

1 cup heavy cream

3 tablespoons chopped fresh
   flat-leaf parsley

2 medium eggs, plus 1 egg yolk,
   whisked

Serves 6

Preheat the oven to 400°F. Liberally butter an 8-inch cake pan, 2 inches deep, with a removable base and dust it with grated Parmesan. You will need to cook the mushrooms in about four batches. Heat a quarter of the remaining butter with a tablespoon of olive oil in a large frying pan, add some of the chopped shallots, and once they have softened add a quarter of the mushrooms. Fry them, stirring frequently, until they soften and start to color, seasoning them towards the end. Move them to a bowl and cook the remainder in the same fashion.

Transfer half of the cooked mushrooms to a food processor and reduce to a textured purée. Combine this with the rest of the mushrooms in a large bowl. Stir in the cream, parsley, eggs, half the remaining Parmesan, and some seasoning.

Transfer this mixture to the prepared pan, scatter the remaining Parmesan on top, and bake for 35–40 minutes, until golden on the surface and set. I like the torte best about 10 minutes out of the oven, though it can also be eaten at room temperature. Run a knife around the collar to remove it, and serve in wedges.

Large pumpkins baked in this fashion make for a full-on earthy, rustic extravaganza. But the bigger they get the more at risk you are of them bursting at the sides as they cook, which is a very messy business. This bijou take plays it safe with baby pumpkins, and you get your very own to dip into, which is always a plus. Basically any small round thick-skinned pumpkin or squash weighing about 1 pound will do.

fondue-filled baby pumpkins

Pumpkins

4 x 1 pound pumpkins or squashes

1 heaped teaspoon cornstarch

2 tablespoons kirsch or white wine

⅔ cup heavy cream

sea salt, black pepper

freshly grated nutmeg

2 cups grated Emmental

2 cups grated Gruyère

Croutons

4 x ½-inch slices day-old white bread,
   crusts removed and diced

extra virgin olive oil

a pinch of dried oregano
   or other dried herb

Serves 4

Preheat the oven to 400°F. Cut the tops off the pumpkins and scoop out the seeds, and if necessary cut a small slice off the bottom so they sit firmly when placed upright, without tipping over. Blend the cornstarch with the kirsch or wine, then stir this into the cream and season with salt, pepper, and nutmeg. Blend this with the grated cheese in a large bowl and use to fill the pumpkins by about two-thirds. Replace the lids, set them inside a baking or roasting dish, and bake for 45 minutes.

In the meantime, scatter the diced bread over the base of a roasting pan, drizzle over a little olive oil, and toss with your hands to lightly coat. Scatter over a little oregano and toast in the oven for 8–10 minutes, until lightly golden.

Remove the lids from the cooked pumpkins, spoon off any butter on the surface, and give the fondue a stir. Pile the croutons into the center and serve immediately, spooning the pumpkin flesh away from the skin and eating it with the fondue.

A clafoutis is classically a sweet dessert set with black cherries or prunes. But ultimately it's just a batter dessert, and the ingredients are the same as for toad-in-the-hole or Yorkshire pudding, and therefore there is no reason why we cannot borrow and set it with savory treasures like strips of grilled zucchini and bits of bacon. It easily translates to a vegetarian main course by adding diced medium-mature goat cheese in lieu of the sautéed bacon.

zucchini, smoky bacon, and rosemary clafoutis

Batter

1 cup all-purpose flour, sifted

½ teaspoon sea salt

2 medium eggs

⅔ cup milk

⅔ cup water

2 teaspoons Dijon mustard

2 teaspoons wholegrain mustard

Filling

3 zucchini, ends trimmed,
    sliced lengthways

extra virgin olive oil

sea salt, black pepper

½ pound bacon, diced

1 tablespoon finely chopped
    fresh rosemary

Serves 4

Blend all the ingredients for the batter together in a blender until smooth, then leave to rest for 30 minutes.

In the meantime, heat a ridged grill pan over medium heat. Brush one side of the zucchini slices with oil, season, and grill for about 3 minutes until lightly colored. Brush the top side with oil, turn, and grill this side for about 2 minutes. They need to color, without being too dark, since they will color further in the oven. You will probably need to cook them in batches.

Also while the batter is resting, heat a large frying pan over medium heat, and add the bacon. Fry for 7–8 minutes, stirring occasionally, until lightly colored and again not too dark, then remove the pan from the heat.

Halfway through resting the batter, preheat the oven to 425°F. Place a couple of tablespoons of oil in a 12-inch oval gratin dish or other dish of a similar size, and heat this in the oven for 10 minutes. Pour the batter into a bowl and stir in the rosemary and half the bacon. Pour this into the dish, then scatter over the zucchini slices, pushing down so about half of them are submerged. Scatter over the remaining bacon, and bake for 30 minutes, until the batter is risen and golden. Serve immediately.

It is easy enough to see why the Italians go overboard about this dark-green bubbly cabbage, which has a really elegant depth to it. Unlike other cabbages, however, even the finest stalks remain stringy on cooking, so it is important to strip the leaves off them completely.

orecchiette with cavolo nero and chicken livers

approx. 1¾ pounds cavolo nero or kale

⅔ pound orecchiette

2–3 tablespoons extra virgin olive oil

4 garlic cloves, peeled and
    finely chopped

sea salt, black pepper

a pinch of dried chile flakes

¾ cup freshly grated Parmesan, plus
    extra to serve

approx. ⅔ pound chicken livers,
    membranes removed, lobes halved
    if large

Serves 4

Strip the leafy parts of the cavolo nero off the stalks, right up to the tips. Slice the leaves across about 1 inch thick and wash.

Bring two large pots of salted water to a boil. Add the cavolo nero to one, cover and simmer for 3 minutes, then drain into a colander, and press out any excess water—a potato masher is good for this. Add the orecchiette to the other pot and simmer for 12–14 minutes or according to the package instructions until just tender. Drain the orecchiette, but not too dry, reserving ½ cup of cooking water, and return the pasta to the pot.

Five minutes before the end of cooking the pasta, heat 2 tablespoons of oil in a large frying pan over medium heat, add the garlic, and fry briefly until fragrant and just starting to color, then add the drained cavolo nero, season with salt and the chile flakes, and fry for a couple of minutes, turning occasionally.

Mix the cavolo nero into the drained pasta. Add the Parmesan, a little seasoning, and a drop of the reserved cooking water and heat, turning it now and then, until it appears coated in a creamy emulsion. You can add a little more water if necessary.

Heat a drop of oil in a clean frying pan over high heat, add the chicken livers, season, and briefly sear each side, leaving them pink and creamy in the center. Mix them into the pasta and accompany with more Parmesan.

gorgeous grains

Grains are only just beginning to reveal the full extent of their talents in the kitchen. For years they've been boxed into a corner, as starchy asides to rib-sticking stews; pearl barley and its type are rarely sold with more advice than "good in soups" on the package, when like most other grains they are good for so much more. Lightly dressed with a vinaigrette, with perhaps some sliced mushrooms and chopped dill, toasted pumpkin and sunflower seeds, or shredded leaves, green beans, and mint, grains redefine our take on the carbohydrate element within a meal. Most will also make fabulous risottos.

Spelt is one of the great underrated grains—gorgeously smooth and plump when cooked, it can be used in exactly the same way as barley. Confusingly it is often equated with farro, but cooks up very differently. While farro requires soaking and always remains firm and chewy, spelt can be cooked like rice and turns creamy and yielding by comparison (which is all very convenient for the time-challenged amongst us). It's lovely stuff that laps up the juices of roasted vegetables, for serving warm or as a salad when the two are newly cooled.

Quinoa is another favorite, one that wholly deserves to become the next big thing, yet it sits on the fringes of mainstream cooking. These tiny buff-colored discs the size of a couscous grain have a really deep, satisfyingly bitter and nutty flavor, and a texture quite unlike any other, courtesy of the fine C-shaped tail or germ that separates from the seed when it cooks. Firmer than couscous, it is still exquisitely delicate. It is in fact a pseudograin, the edible seeds of a species of goosefoot, and not a grass at all. But just as we treat avocados and tomatoes as vegetables rather than fruits, so too quinoa has joined the grain gang in the kitchen.

Spelt, like pearl barley, makes for the most warming and nourishing of hearty soups. It relishes the likes of bacon and cabbage, and a shower of Parmesan added at the end.

wintery spelt soup

2 tomatoes

2 tablespoons extra virgin olive oil

⅓ pound pancetta or bacon, diced

3 garlic cloves, peeled and finely chopped

1 teaspoon finely sliced medium-hot red chile

½ cup pearled spelt, rinsed

5 cups chicken or vegetable stock

½ small Savoy cabbage (approx. 10 ounces), cut into wide strips, tough white parts discarded

6 tablespoons coarsely chopped fresh flat-leaf parsley, plus extra to serve

sea salt

freshly grated Parmesan to serve

Serves 4

Bring a large pan of water to a boil. Cut out a cone from the top of each tomato, dunk them into the boiling water for about 20 seconds, and then into cold water. Slip off the skins and chop the flesh.

Heat the olive oil in a large saucepan over medium heat. Add the pancetta or bacon and fry for 5–8 minutes until lightly golden, stirring occasionally, then add the garlic and chile and cook for a minute longer until fragrant. Add the chopped tomatoes and cook for a few minutes longer until mushy, then stir in the spelt. Add the stock, bring to a boil, and simmer for 20 minutes, adding the cabbage after 15 minutes. Stir in the parsley and salt for taste. Serve with extra parsley scattered on top, accompanied by Parmesan.

There are few better ways of enjoying the first peas of summer. Though given the brevity of the season, ready-shelled peas will make a fine stand-in for shell-on peas at any other time. This is half soup, half risotto, and all the stock is added in one go so there's no hanging around the stove.

venetian peas and rice

4 tablespoons unsalted butter

1 small onion, peeled and chopped

2 cups fresh shelled peas

1 cup risotto rice

⅔ cup white wine

4 cups fresh vegetable stock

sea salt, black pepper

⅓ cup freshly grated Parmesan

4 tablespoons coarsely chopped fresh
flat-leaf parsley, plus extra to serve

Serves 4

Heat the butter and onion in a large saucepan and cook until the onion is lightly colored. Add the peas and rice and stir for a minute or two. Now add the wine, stock, and seasoning, bring to a simmer, cover, and cook for 15 minutes, by which time the rice should be tender. Stir in the Parmesan and 4 tablespoons of parsley and adjust the seasoning. Scatter each bowl with a little extra parsley and serve immediately, although this is more accommodating than a risotto and will sit around for a few minutes if you're not quite ready to eat.

Delicious dished up with a spicy chutney or syrupy balsamic onions, and die-hard meat-lovers could stir in some little bits of chorizo (allow about ⅔ cup).

bulgar wheat, cashew nut, and arugula pilaf

3 tablespoons extra virgin olive oil

1 large onion, peeled and chopped

1 teaspoon ground cumin

1 teaspoon ground coriander

a pinch of dried chile flakes

3 garlic cloves, peeled and finely chopped

3 strips lemon zest (removed
   with a potato peeler)

1 tablespoon fresh thyme leaves

1 bay leaf

2 cups bulgar wheat

⅔ cup white wine

2 cups fresh chicken or vegetable stock

sea salt

½ cup arugula, leaves cut in half

1 cup roasted cashews

sour cream to serve

Serves 6

Heat the olive oil in a medium saucepan over medium heat. Add the onion and fry for 5–8 minutes until lightly colored, stirring occasionally. Add the spices, garlic, lemon zest, and herbs, give everything a stir and cook for 1 minute longer. Add the bulgar wheat and give it a stir, then add the wine, stock, and some salt, bring to a boil and simmer over low heat for 8 minutes. Remove from the heat, cover, and leave to stand for 20 minutes. Discard the bay leaf and lemon zest, add the arugula and cashews, and toss. Serve with sour cream.

Butternut squash cooks up like pumpkin but is denser and sweeter, and has the edge in a risotto where it holds its shape. It goes so well with sage, it is hard to deviate to any other herb.

butternut squash and sage risotto

2 tablespoons extra virgin olive oil

1 x 1½ pound butternut squash, skin and seeds removed, thickly sliced

sea salt, black pepper

5 cups fresh chicken or vegetable stock

7 tablespoons unsalted butter

1 onion, peeled and finely chopped

2 garlic cloves, peeled and finely chopped

1½ cups risotto rice

⅔ cup white wine

½ cup freshly grated Parmesan

a large handful of fresh sage leaves

Serves 4

Heat the olive oil in a large frying pan over medium heat. Add enough squash to cover the base of the pan (you will probably need to do this in two batches), season, and color on either side.

Bring the stock to a boil in a small saucepan with some seasoning, and keep it at a simmer at the back of the stove, half covered with a lid. Heat half the butter in a medium heavy-bottomed saucepan over medium heat and sweat the onion and garlic for several minutes, until glossy and relaxed. Add the rice and stir for a minute or two until it is translucent and coated in butter. Add the wine, and once this has been absorbed add the squash and give everything a good stir. Now start to add the stock a few ladles at a time—the rice should be just covered but not flooded. The risotto should take 20–25 minutes to cook once you start to add the liquid, and by the end the squash should be tender. Remove the pan from the heat while the grains still have some resistance, leaving it on the sloppy side. Stir in the Parmesan and taste for seasoning.

Just before the risotto is ready, melt the remaining butter in a medium frying pan over medium heat. Once the foam subsides, add the sage leaves and fry for a few minutes until pale and crisp. Serve the risotto on warm plates, with the sage leaves and butter spooned over.

Baby leeks have all the flavor you might want from the mature vegetable but with a more delicate texture. This opens all sorts of doors when serving them: salads for instance, or lightly blanched as a little end garnish.

oven-baked saffron risotto with spring vegetables

Risotto

4 cups chicken or vegetable stock

3½ tablespoons unsalted butter

1 onion, peeled and finely chopped

1½ cups risotto rice

⅔ cups white wine

a pinch of saffron filaments (approx. 20),
   ground and blended with 1 tablespoon
   boiling water

sea salt, black pepper

½ cup freshly grated Parmesan, plus
   extra to serve

On Top

6 slices of prosciutto, halved lengthways

1 tablespoon unsalted butter

½ teaspoon superfine sugar

6 baby leeks, trimmed and sliced
   diagonally into 1–inch pieces

5 ounces fresh shelled peas

5 ounces snow peas, tops trimmed

Serves 4

Preheat the oven to 375°F. Bring the stock to a boil in a small saucepan. Melt half the butter in a medium cast iron casserole over medium heat and fry the onion for a few minutes until translucent. Stir in the rice and cook for 1–2 minutes, stirring occasionally. Add the wine and continue to cook until absorbed, then add the saffron liquid, the stock, and plenty of seasoning. Bring to a boil, cover, and cook in the oven for 25 minutes.

In the meantime, heat the broiler, lay the prosciutto on a broiler pan and cook until the fat starts to buckle and appear crisp. This happens quite quickly, so keep an eye on it. Turn and cook the other side.

Ten minutes before the risotto is ready, bring ⅔ cup of water to a boil in a small saucepan over medium heat with the butter, sugar, and ½ teaspoon of salt. Add the leeks, cover, and cook for 2 minutes, then stir in the peas and snow peas, cover, and cook for another 2–4 minutes, until the vegetables are just tender. Drain them into a sieve.

Stir the remaining butter and ½ cup Parmesan into the risotto. It should be a lovely thick dropping consistency, but if necessary you can stir in a tad more hot stock. Serve with the vegetables spooned on top, a little extra Parmesan scattered on top, and the grilled prosciutto.

This oven-baked risotto is wonderfully luxurious, with no stinting on the butter; laced with capers, it melts over the scallops at the end. Should you be fortunate enough to find scallops with their corals attached, around twelve should do. To prepare them, pull the coral away from the meat and with it the surrounding girdle and white gristle (cut off and discard these). Depending on the size of your oven, you will probably need to roast the onions in advance of cooking the risotto.

oven-baked roasted onion risotto with scallops

1½ pounds red onions, peeled, halved, and thickly sliced

extra virgin olive oil

sea salt, black pepper

3½ tablespoons unsalted butter, softened

2 garlic cloves, peeled and crushed to a paste

1½ cups risotto rice

⅔ cup white wine

5 cups chicken or vegetable stock

1 heaping tablespoon capers

3 tablespoons coarsely chopped fresh flat-leaf parsley

½ teaspoon finely grated lemon zest, plus a squeeze of juice

16 large scallops

½ cup freshly grated Parmesan

Serves 4

Preheat the oven to 400°F. Scatter the onion slices over the base of one or two roasting dishes in a crowded single layer, drizzle with 3 tablespoons of olive oil, season with a little salt, and roast for 30–45 minutes until golden, stirring halfway through. Set aside.

Melt half the butter in a large cast-iron casserole over medium heat, add the garlic, and stir until you get a heady hit of garlic butter. Add the rice and stir for about 1 minute, then pour in the wine, and simmer until almost completely absorbed. Pour in the stock and season, bring to a boil, cover, and cook in the oven for 25 minutes. In the meantime blend the remaining butter with the capers, parsley, lemon zest, and juice.

About 10 minutes before the risotto is ready, heat a large non-stick frying pan over high heat. Toss the scallops with oil to coat them, then season and sear for 1–1½ minutes each side until caramelized; they should give slightly when you press them. You will need to cook them in two batches.

Stir the Parmesan and onions into the rice, and top with the scallops. Pop the remaining butter into the scallop pan and once it appears semi-melted spoon this over the risotto and serve immediately.

Cultivated in the Andes for over 6,000 years, the Incas referred to quinoa as "the mother of all grains." And well they might, since it contains more protein than any other grain, and unlike wheat and rice can boast all the essential amino acids, and is gluten-free.

It stands in for bulgar to make a fine tabbouleh, perfect mid-summer when tomatoes are at their best; you could use any that promise to be really sweet and juicy. Try to buy your herbs in nice big bunches, and use just the tender young leaves.

quinoa, feta, and herb salad

1 cup quinoa

3 tablespoons lemon juice

sea salt, black pepper

8 tablespoons extra virgin olive oil

½ cup young fresh mint leaves, coarsely chopped

1½ cups young fresh flat-leaf parsley leaves, coarsely chopped

1½ cups cherry tomatoes, halved or quartered depending on their size

6 scallions, trimmed and thinly sliced

7 ounces feta, cut into ½-inch dice

Serves 4–6

Bring a medium pan of salted water to a boil. Heat a large frying pan over medium heat, scatter the quinoa over the base and toast for a few minutes, stirring frequently, until it gives off a lovely warm aroma and starts popping. Transfer to a bowl and leave to cool for a few minutes, then add to the boiling water and simmer for 15–20 minutes until tender. Drain into a sieve, return it to the saucepan, cover, and leave to cool.

Whisk the lemon juice with 2 tablespoons of water and some seasoning in a small bowl, then whisk in the oil. Combine the herbs in a large bowl with the tomatoes, scallions, and cooled quinoa. You can prepare the salad to this point up to a couple of hours in advance. Shortly before serving add the dressing and toss, then gently mix in the feta.

This salad just sings with goodness. I love to toss tart sweet fruits into tabbouleh—mango slivers, red currants, or pomegranate seeds, as well as grapes. As with the salad on page 105, your parsley needs to be young and tender, so avoid any overgrown bunches. Should you have any tabbouleh left over, seal the surface with a lettuce leaf and cover with plastic wrap.

tabbouleh with grapes

1½ tablespoons fine bulgar*

2½ cups fresh flat-leaf parsley,
   tough stalks removed

2 tomatoes, sliced and then chopped

a handful of fresh mint leaves, chopped

1 large scallion, finely sliced
   and then chopped

sea salt, black pepper

3 tablespoons extra virgin olive oil

2 tablespoons lemon juice

½ cup each of red and white seedless
   grapes, halved

Serves 4

Rinse the bulgar in a fine-mesh sieve and leave it on the side to absorb the remaining moisture. Chop the parsley, starting at the leaf end and working towards the stalk. Combine the parsley, tomatoes, mint, and scallion in a bowl, then add some seasoning, olive oil, and lemon juice and combine. Mix in the bulgar and the grapes, reserving a few to scatter over at the end, then pile the salad on to a plate or dish.

*Fine bulgar is available from Middle Eastern delis. Alternatively blend ordinary bulgar wheat in a coffee grinder until about half the size.

Red rice is lovely stuff—nutty and aromatic, it lends itself more readily to salads than white rice. This serves as a side dish within a selection of salads, perhaps to some grilled chicken escalopes or other small tasty cut.

red rice salad

1¼ cups red rice
2 tablespoons lemon juice
4 tablespoons extra virgin olive oil
2 tablespoons finely chopped shallots
8 tablespoons mixed finely chopped
    fresh flat-leaf parsley, mint, basil,
    and dill
sea salt, black pepper

Serves 4–6

Bring a large pot of salted water to a boil. Add the rice and simmer for 30–35 minutes until tender, then drain into a sieve or colander, and run cold water through it. Toss the rice in a bowl with the lemon juice, olive oil, shallots, herbs, and some seasoning.

A dollop of garlicky yogurt provides a little luxury—blend 1 cup of Greek yogurt with a small crushed garlic clove or two, a little salt, and a pinch of sugar. It strikes just the right note alongside a joint of rare seared beef or lamb.

couscous with green beans, mint, and lemon

sea salt

5 tablespoons extra virgin olive oil

1½ cups couscous

½ pound fine French beans,
stalk ends removed

½ pound sugar snap peas, stalk ends
removed

2 tablespoons lemon juice

a handful of fresh mint leaves, torn

2 tablespoons finely diced
preserved lemon

Serves 6

Bring a large pot of salted water to a boil for the beans. At the same time bring 2 cups of water to a boil in a medium saucepan with a little salt and 1 tablespoon of oil. Add the couscous and simmer for 1 minute. Cover with a tightly fitting lid and leave to stand for 10 minutes.

Halfway into this time add the beans to the large pot of boiling water, cook for 2 minutes, then add the sugar snaps and cook for another 2 minutes. Drain into a sieve and leave for a few minutes for the surface moisture to evaporate.

Fluff up the couscous with a fork, then mix in the beans and sugar snaps. Blend the lemon juice with a little salt, add the remaining oil, and pour this dressing over the couscous. Serve with the torn mint and the preserved lemon scattered on top. This salad can be served warm or cold.

Spelt laps up the juices from roasted peppers, but butternut squash roasted with cherry tomatoes and lots of red onions is another mélange that would welcome the grain. Cooked spelt is extraordinarily good-natured, and unlike most grains that continue to absorb a salad dressing once it's mixed in, this is in much the same condition the day after you make it. It's worth, though, holding back on tossing in the basil leaves until close to the time of serving, to ensure they remain suitably perky.

roasted pepper, spelt, and pistachio salad

7 long red peppers, core and seeds removed, halved lengthways, and cut into wide strips
1 medium-hot red chile, core and seeds removed, cut into long thin strips
7 tablespoons extra virgin olive oil
sea salt
3 red onions, peeled, halved, and thickly sliced
4 garlic cloves, peeled and sliced
2 tablespoons balsamic vinegar
7 ounces (approx. 1 cup) pearled spelt
a handful of fresh basil leaves, torn
¼ cup shelled pistachio nuts

Serves 6

Preheat the oven to 425°F. Arrange the peppers and chile strips in a crowded single layer in a roasting dish. Drizzle over 4 tablespoons of olive oil and season with salt. Roast for 40–50 minutes, stirring in the onions after 20 minutes, and the garlic after 30 minutes. Everything should be nicely golden at the edges by the end. When the peppers come out of the oven, drizzle over the vinegar and remaining olive oil and leave to cool.

At the same time bring a large pot of salted water to a boil, add the spelt and simmer for 15–20 minutes until just tender. Drain into a sieve, then return it to the pot, cover, and leave to cool.

Mix the spelt into the peppers and onions, and add the basil and pistachios.

Inspiration for this comes from UP or Urban Picnic, a boutique lunch take-out in East London—they complete this particular line-up of salads with roasted or barbecued butterflied lamb rubbed with sumac.

barley salad with honeyed tomatoes and dates

Barley Salad

⅔ cup pearl barley

1 teaspoon coriander seeds

½ tablespoon red wine vinegar

sea salt, black pepper

4 tablespoons extra virgin olive oil

¼ cup pitted black olives, halved
   lengthways

a few handfuls of arugula leaves

Zucchini

2 zucchini, ends removed, cut into
   long thin strips

extra virgin olive oil

Tomato Salad

2 teaspoons honey

1 tablespoon lemon juice

3 tablespoons extra virgin olive oil

7 ounces cocktail plum tomatoes, e.g.
   Marzinino, quartered lengthways

⅔ cup Medjool dates, stoned and
   quartered lengthways

Serves 4

Bring a large pot of salted water to a boil, add the barley, and simmer for 40–45 minutes or until tender. Drain into a sieve, return to the pot, cover, and leave to cool.

Heat a small frying pan over medium heat and briefly toast the coriander seeds, then coarsely grind them using a pestle and mortar. Whisk the vinegar with some seasoning, then whisk in the oil, and stir in the coriander. Toss the barley with the dressing and mix in the olives. You can prepare the salad to this point several hours in advance.

Heat a ridged grill pan over medium-high heat. Take as many zucchini slices as will fit the grill pan, brush them with olive oil on one side, and season. Grill this side for 3–5 minutes until striped with gold, then brush the other side with oil, turn, and grill this side too. Remove them to a plate and grill the remainder in the same fashion. Leave the slices to cool—you can cook them well in advance.

Whisk the honey, lemon juice, and some seasoning in a small bowl, then whisk in the oil. Toss with the tomatoes and dates in a bowl.

Toss in the arugula just before eating and serve with the grilled zucchini and tomato salad.

potatoes

Little is more comforting in times of trouble than a thick potato soup. And you can't use new or red potatoes for this, as later potatoes with their loose mealy consistency is ideal for melting into a rich stock. This wholesome leek and potato soup is one of the backbones of my kitchen, that I make by the large potful whenever anyone in the family is feeling below par. While sweet potatoes that cook to a beautiful melting softness make for a deliciously aromatic and velvety soup that's just as soothing.

We are rarely starved of waxy-fleshed or "new" potatoes these days, even in the midst of winter, which makes potato salads a year-round treat. But there is no beating the summer crop of first earlies, defined by their papery skin that doesn't need peeling so much as tending with a scrubbing brush. The recalcitrant flakes left clinging are a part of their charm and imperceptible in eating. Thicker than this and I do peel them, but not the real tiny ones which would disappear down the sink.

My favorite potato salad contains a mass of freshly chopped tender herbs. Dressed while warm the potatoes actually improve if you leave the salad overnight, something that always appeals to lazy cooks who hate doing everything at the last minute, and is useful if you are planning a barbecue or Sunday lunch. The other magic ingredient for any potato salad is a little onion, added judiciously, and it's stardust. Scallions are raised for the job, red onions are sweeter and milder than white ones, and finely chopped shallot will fire things up nicely too. But if you want to be really subtle, slip a few drops of onion juice, squeezed through a garlic press, into the dressing instead.

A completely different animal from vichyssoise, mealy, wholesome, and nicely slippery. Children of all ages adore this soup, and it's one that I crave when feeling in any way delicate—it nurtures perfectly. It's also good for Sunday night if you've got a pot of homemade chicken stock sitting on the stove; quite likely you will have the other ingredients in house too. The bacon of course isn't *de rigueur*.

leek and potato soup

3½ tablespoons unsalted butter

1½ pounds leeks (trimmed weight), sliced

1 large onion, peeled and chopped

1 cup white wine

5½ cups fresh chicken or vegetable stock

approx. ⅓ pound potatoes, peeled and thinly sliced

sea salt, black pepper

½ pound bacon, diced

snipped fresh chives

Serves 6

Melt the butter in a large saucepan over medium-low heat and sweat the leeks and onion for 8–10 minutes, without coloring, until they are silky and soft, stirring them occasionally. Add the wine and reduce until syrupy. Meanwhile bring the stock to a boil in a separate pan. Add the sliced potatoes to the leeks and stir them around for 1 minute, then pour in the boiling stock, season, and simmer for 8 minutes.

At the same time, heat a frying pan over medium-low heat, add the bacon, and fry for 7–8 minutes, until it is dark and crisp, stirring occasionally. Transfer it to a bowl with a slotted spoon.

Blitz the soup in batches in a food processor to a textured consistency. Return it to a clean saucepan, taste to check the seasoning, and gently reheat. Ladle the soup into warm bowls, scatter the bacon and chives on top, and serve.

As thick, comforting, and mealy as you would hope a sweet potato soup to be. And it's the orange-fleshed potatoes you want here rather than the cream-colored ones. The Roquefort is particularly good with all that sweetness, but it could just as well be shreds of chorizo or little croutons.

sweet potato and rosemary soup

extra virgin olive oil

1 large onion, peeled and chopped

1 heaping tablespoon fresh rosemary leaves

4 garlic cloves, peeled and finely chopped

a pinch of dried chile flakes

2 pounds orange-fleshed sweet potatoes, peeled and thickly sliced

5 cups fresh chicken or vegetable stock

sea salt

½-¾ cup Roquefort, crumbled

Serves 4–6

Heat 3 tablespoons of olive oil in a large saucepan over medium heat. Add the onion and rosemary and fry for 3–5 minutes until relaxed and glossy, stirring occasionally. Add the garlic and chile and fry for a minute or two longer. Add the sweet potatoes and continue to cook for another couple of minutes, stirring frequently. Pour in the stock and season with salt, then bring to a boil and simmer over low heat for 20 minutes, by which time the potato should be meltingly tender. Pureé the soup in batches and pass through a sieve. Return it to the saucepan and season with a little more salt if necessary. The soup can be prepared well in advance.

Reheat if necessary, and serve in warm bowls. Scatter the Roquefort on top—most of this will sink and melt, but a little should peek out at the top. Drizzle over a little olive oil and serve.

There is something very dated about baked potatoes. But they are very tasty, and this James Bond-like preference for "crushed not mashed" seeks to bring them forward to the present day.

What are sold as baking potatoes are not so much special varieties as potatoes of a particular size—they should be ½ pound in weight. There are usually one or two potatoes in an ordinary pack that will be large enough for baking. These can be filled and then chilled until required and reheated.

crushed not mashed

Potatoes
4 baking potatoes
extra virgin olive oil
coarse-grain sea salt

Filling
2 heaping tablespoons coarsely chopped
   fresh flat-leaf parsley
½ garlic clove, peeled and crushed
sea salt, black pepper

Serves 4

Preheat the oven to 350°F. Scrub the potatoes and dry them. Make an incision the shape of a lid on the top of each one with a small sharp knife. Pour a little olive oil into the palm of your hand and rub your hands together and then over the potatoes, lightly coating each one with oil. Place them in a baking dish, sprinkle with some crystals of sea salt, and bake for 1½ hours, until the skin is rich and crisp and the insides are fluffy.

Use a spoon to remove the potato from the skins and roughly crush with a fork. Combine with 5 tablespoons of olive oil, the chopped parsley, garlic, and seasoning, and refill.

Sautéd potatoes are the fries of the home, arguably more delicious with all those crispy little bits, and it's worth cooking them skin-on for this. Butter combined with olive oil gives you the best of both worlds, as you get that lovely flavor without the risk of burning, but you can vary this, and goose fat is always a promise of a fabulous result. It's worth taking your time—frying the potatoes slowly allows the sugars to caramelize. The fried onions turn them into Lyonnaise potatoes, but you can go on building: fried wild mushrooms, broiled bacon, poached eggs.

lyonnaise potatoes

1½ pounds new or red potatoes, scrubbed

2 tablespoons unsalted butter

3 tablespoons extra virgin olive oil

sea salt, black pepper

1 garlic clove, peeled and finely chopped

2 tablespoons finely chopped fresh
   flat-leaf parsley

2 large onions (ideally white), peeled,
   halved, and finely sliced

1 teaspoon red wine vinegar

Serves 3–4

Bring a large pan of salted water to a boil, add the potatoes, and cook for 15–20 minutes until tender when pierced with a knife. Drain them into a colander, leave to cool, then slice them thickly.

Heat the butter and 1 tablespoon of olive oil in a large frying pan over low heat and sauté the potatoes for about 20 minutes, turning them every few minutes or so, until they are evenly golden and crisp, seasoning them a few minutes into cooking. Five minutes towards the end, add the chopped garlic. Finally sprinkle the chopped parsley on top and toss to distribute it.

At the same time as frying the potatoes, heat the remaining olive oil in a large frying pan over low heat, and gently fry the onions for 20–25 minutes, stirring frequently until they are evenly gold and sweet. At the very end, season them with salt, pepper, and the red wine vinegar. Toss them into the sautéd potatoes and serve immediately.

Feta tossed into small crispy roasted potatoes at the end of their cooking time just melts and softens, and the herbs broaden out their appeal. Take advantage of any soft herbs you have growing in the garden, also the pale green leafy fronds on the inside of fennel bulbs or celery hearts. You could just about get away with settling down to a plate of these without a roast in tow, which you would be hard pressed to do with normal roasted potatoes. You can peel the potatoes or leave them unpeeled if you prefer, they will be equally good in a rustic fashion.

crispy roasties with feta

2¾ pounds medium new potatoes, peeled or unpeeled, halved lengthways

3 tablespoons extra virgin olive oil

sea salt

7 ounces feta, diced

2 tablespoons coarsely chopped fresh flat-leaf parsley

2 tablespoons snipped fresh chives

Serves 6

Heat the oven to 425°F. Bring a large pot of salted water to a boil, add the potatoes, and cook for 10 minutes. Drain into a colander and leave for a few minutes for the surface moisture to evaporate, then return them to the pot and give them a vigorous shake. Add the olive oil and toss, and season with salt. Tip these into a large roasting dish, so they fit in a crowded single layer. Roast for 1 hour, stirring them halfway through. Stir in the feta and return to the oven for 5 minutes, then scatter the herbs on top and serve.

This has lots and lots of fresh herbs in it, and you can use whatever you have growing. The potatoes are dressed warm, and infuse with the lively scents—in fact it's even better left overnight.

a stock favorite
potato salad

1½ pounds small new potatoes, peeled
   or scrubbed

Dressing
2 tablespoons white wine
9 tablespoons extra virgin olive oil
4 tablespoons chopped fresh herbs,
   e.g. parsley, chives, basil,
   chervil, tarragon
2 scallions, trimmed and finely sliced
sea salt, black pepper

Serves 4–6

Lay the potatoes in the top half of a steamer set over a little boiling water in the lower half, cover, and cook until tender. Rinse the steamer under cold water to wash off the sticky starch on the surface of the potatoes. Alternatively bring a large pot of salted water to a boil, add the potatoes, cook for 15–20 minutes until tender when a skewer is inserted, then drain into a colander.

Thickly slice the hot potatoes, place in a bowl, and pour over the wine and olive oil. Gently toss in the herbs, scallions, and some seasoning. Leave to cool to room temperature. If not serving immediately, cover and chill. In this case bring back to room temperature for 30 minutes before serving.

The iodine-rich flavor of anchovies is gracefully absorbed by the sweetness of the potatoes. With slivers of red onion in there too, this is quite a bold potato salad, and as ever with anchovies the mind strays to tomatoes and olives, or even some lightly cooked eggs.

potato, anchovy, and red onion salad

2 pounds medium new potatoes,
   peeled and halved if large
9 tablespoons extra virgin olive oil
1 tablespoon lemon juice
sea salt, black pepper
8 anchovy fillets, thinly sliced across
1 red onion, peeled, halved
   and thinly sliced
4 tablespoons coarsely chopped
   fresh flat-leaf parsley

Serves 4

Bring a large pot of salted water to a boil, add the potatoes, and simmer for 15–20 minutes until tender when a skewer is inserted. Drain them into a colander and leave to cool for about 10 minutes. Halve or quarter them depending on their size and place in a large bowl. Pour over the olive oil and lemon juice and season them, then fold in the remaining ingredients. Leave the salad to cool completely.

This can also be made a day in advance, covered, and chilled, in which case fold in the parsley just before serving, and bring back to room temperature for 30 minutes before eating.

potato salad with roquefort and walnuts

Salad

1½ pounds small new potatoes, peeled
  or scrubbed

¾ cup walnut halves

1 large or 2 small heads of chicory

1 celery heart, outer sticks discarded
  and finely sliced

2 scallions, trimmed and thinly
  sliced

7 ounces Roquefort

a handful of watercress sprigs

Dressing

1 tablespoon red wine vinegar

a squeeze of lemon juice

1 scant teaspoon Dijon mustard

sea salt, black pepper

4 tablespoons walnut oil

4 tablespoons peanut oil

Serves 4–6

Lay the potatoes in the top half of a steamer set over a little boiling water in the lower half, cover, and cook until tender. Rinse the steamer under cold water to wash off the sticky starch on the surface of the potatoes. Alternatively bring a large pot of salted water to a boil, add the potatoes, cook for 15–20 minutes until tender when a skewer is inserted, then drain into a colander. Leave the potatoes to cool while you assemble the remaining ingredients.

Roughly break the walnut halves into 2 or 3 pieces. Heat a frying pan over medium heat and toast them for 3 minutes, tossing constantly to ensure they don't burn. Transfer them to a bowl or plate and leave to cool. Trim the base of the chicory bulbs and remove the outer leaves. Halve them, cut out the inner core, and slice into long thin strips. Whisk the vinegar and lemon juice in a small bowl with the mustard and some seasoning, then whisk in the oils.

Place the potatoes in a large bowl, pour the dressing over, and gently turn to coat them. Now mix in the celery, scallions, chicory, and walnuts. Using your fingers, crumble the Roquefort into cubes about ½ inch in size and gently fold them into the salad to avoid mushing them up. Finally toss in the watercress. Pile the salad on to a large serving dish, or individual plates.

Color is everything here: the potatoes are dyed a sunny gold by the saffron. They should be big enough to peel without disappearing, but small enough to leave whole. And as ever, unless you are using very young fava beans that can be eaten skin and all, frozen baby ones might be a better bet, otherwise it's best to peel them.

saffron potato and bean salad

¼ teaspoon saffron filaments, ground

1¾ pounds small new potatoes

½ pound baby fava beans

⅓ pound sugar snap peas, stalk ends removed

2 tablespoons white wine

9 tablespoons extra virgin olive oil

sea salt, black pepper

a couple of squeezes of lemon juice

4 tablespoons coarsely chopped fresh flat-leaf parsley

Serves 6–8

Bring just enough salted water to cover the potatoes to a boil in a medium saucepan. Add a little boiling water to the ground saffron, pour the liquor into the pan, and give the water a stir. Add the potatoes and simmer for 15–20 minutes until tender. Drain them into a colander and leave for a few minutes for the surface water to evaporate.

Bring another two medium pans of water to a boil. Add the fava beans to one and simmer for 4–6 minutes, until tender, then drain them into a sieve and briefly run cold water through them. Add the sugar snaps to the other pan, cook for 1 minute, then drain and run cold water through those as well.

Place the warm potatoes in a large bowl and dress with the wine, olive oil, and some seasoning. Toss in the fava beans and sugar snaps. Add a couple of squeezes of lemon juice and leave to cool. Toss in the parsley. If not serving within a couple of hours, cover and chill until required, and bring back to room temperature 1 hour before eating, adding the lemon juice at the last minute.

Fries, known in this case as chips, don't have to be deep-fried to taste good, it's inherent in their shape, and if you boil these potatoes and dress them with a vinaigrette they're pretty good too. So this is a variation on the theme of fish and chips. Any seafood that is good eaten cold can be included—cooked mussels, clams, or squid. Vary the choice according to availability. I like to use nice juicy shrimp, with their tails attached. Should your scallops come "coral-less," then up the number to ten.

fish and chip salad

1½ pounds medium new potatoes, scrubbed or peeled

6 large scallops

6 tablespoons extra virgin olive oil

½ pound cooked shrimp

3 tablespoons caper berries, rinsed and stalks removed

4 tablespoons coarsely chopped fresh flat-leaf parsley

1 tablespoon lemon juice

sea salt

Serves 4

Bring a medium pot of salted water to a boil. Cut the potatoes into ½ inch chips, boil for about 10 minutes until tender, then carefully drain them into a sieve, and leave to cool.

Separate the corals from the scallop meat, pulling off the gristle and skirt with them. Cut off and discard the gristle and slice the scallop meat into thin discs. Heat 1 tablespoon of oil in a large frying pan over high heat, add the scallop discs and corals, and cook for about 30 seconds each side until they turn opaque. Transfer them to a large bowl and leave to cool.

Add the shrimp, caper berries, parsley, the remaining olive oil, lemon juice, and a little salt to the scallops and toss, then gently mix in the potatoes.

big salads

It's as though every decade of late has left a legacy in salads. The Sixties were all about floppy lettuces and salad cream, still a winner when the leaves are carefully prepared and crisped in ice-cold water, and the salad cream is homemade with English mustard and plenty of sugar. The Seventies were a bit bald as it was all rather hale and hearty, while in the Eighties things became a little more interesting, with "warm salads" that bridged the divide between a side salad and a main course—the tender breast of a quail gently wilting a mound of escarole, or the yolk of a lightly poached egg trickling down. And the Nineties was shaped by our love affair with all things Italian, those gorgeous roasted vegetables (see page 24) that we are still avidly pursuing.

Today, however, is all about "BIG" salads, overstated splashes of Renaissance exuberance and color, with all restraint banished. The emphasis, quite rightly, is on allure. I have to fight fingers out of the salad bowl to make sure it is not denuded of crisp snippets of bacon and toasted pine nuts before it reaches the table. Nuts toasted to a crisp, caper berries, and raisins build interest into the equation. I also love that mix of cooked and raw, some leaves thrown in with blanched snow peas, and sharp accents, like lemon and mint, added to slippery fried zucchinis. It's as though salads are going through a rather lovely hippy phase.

One or two of these, prepared well in advance, sitting on the table, and whatever else you choose to dish up with them is a breeze. You can turn to the barbecue, chuck a rib of beef or shoulder of lamb into the oven, or more modestly fry up some sardines or other fish fillets with the simplest marinade—equal quantities of lemon juice and olive oil, some crushed fennel seeds, and a little cayenne pepper is a favorite in our house.

If cauliflower was a different shape then I'm sure we'd be grilling away and eating rather more of it in salads than we do. Still, it works well providing it has a few sparring partners, like pickles and chiles. But don't be tempted to use two small chiles instead of one large one—their size is in inverse ratio to their heat, and you want a nice spicy tang rather than full on hit.

cauliflower, snow peas, chile, and caper berry salad

1 cauliflower, cut into 1-inch florets
   (approx. 1½ pounds)
½ pound snow peas, stalk ends
   trimmed
1½ tablespoons red wine vinegar
1 heaping teaspoon Dijon mustard
1 heaping teaspoon honey
1 garlic clove, peeled and crushed
   to a paste
sea salt
9 tablespoons extra virgin olive oil
1 large fresh red chile, seeds
   discarded and cut into fine strips
caper berries to garnish, stalks
   removed

Serves 6

Bring a large pot of salted water to a boil, add the cauliflower florets, and cook for 6 minutes, then add the snow peas and cook for another 2 minutes. Drain into a colander, briefly run under cold water, then leave to cool.

Transfer the vegetables to a shallow serving dish. Whisk the vinegar, mustard, honey, garlic, and some salt together in a small bowl, then add the oil and whisk until you have a thick creamy emulsion. Scatter the chile strips and caper berries over the salad, drizzle with the dressing, and season with a little more salt.

The spicy crisp almonds serve as a piquant burst of flavor, hard to resist on their own; they toast up well as a snack at any other time.

spinach, cherry tomato, and avocado salad

Nuts

½ cup whole almonds, peeled

1 tablespoon extra virgin olive oil

1 teaspoon dark soy sauce

1 teaspoon fresh thyme leaves

¼ teaspoon cayenne pepper

Salad

2 avocados

¼ pound baby spinach leaves, or
   sliced young spinach leaves

2 tablespoons extra virgin olive oil

a squeeze of lemon juice

7 ounces (1¼ cups) cherry tomatoes
   on the vine, halved

a small handful of fresh chives,
   halved

sea salt

Serves 4–6

Preheat the oven to 375°F. Toss the almonds in a bowl with the olive oil and soy sauce, then toss in the thyme, scatter the cayenne pepper on top, and toss again. Tip the nuts into a small roasting or baking dish and spread them out in a single layer. Toast in the oven for 15–20 minutes, until deep golden and crisp. Transfer the nuts to a plate and leave to cool.

Remove the avocados from the stone in two halves, and pick the stone out. Halve these again into quarters and peel off the skin, then slice each quarter into two long segments. Toss the spinach in a large bowl with the olive oil and lemon juice, then carefully fold in the cherry tomatoes and avocado. Pile the salad on to plates and scatter the spiced nuts and chives on top. Serve immediately, leaving each diner to season their own salad with sea salt.

A wintery mélange: make this around Christmas and you should have the cheeses to go with it, a sliver of something blue and creamy or a flaky mature Cheddar.

salad of red cabbage, apple, and dates

Salad

⅓ cup hazelnuts, peeled and halved

¼ red cabbage (approx. ½ pound)

1 apple, cored and thinly sliced

½ cup Medjool dates, stoned, and
    quartered lengthways

3 scallions, trimmed and
    finely sliced diagonally

Dressing

1 tablespoon red wine vinegar

1 teaspoon Dijon mustard

1 level teaspoon superfine sugar

sea salt, black pepper

3 tablespoons hazelnut oil

3 tablespoons peanut oil

Serves 4

Preheat the oven to 400°F. Place the hazelnuts on a small baking tray and toast them for 8–10 minutes, until lightly golden. Remove and leave to cool. Slice the red cabbage as finely as possible, then halve the strands, and discard any tough white ones.

Whisk the vinegar with the mustard, sugar, and some salt and pepper, then whisk in the oils until you have a creamy emulsified dressing. Toss the red cabbage, apple, dates, and scallions in a bowl. You can do this a couple of hours in advance of eating, in which case cover and set aside. Shortly before serving, mix in half the nuts, re-whisk the dressing if necessary, and drizzle it on top, then scatter the rest of the nuts on top.

Organic and healthfood shops with a fresh vegetable section tend to be the best source for sprouting seeds. Mung beans are particularly good should you be able to find them.

mixed sprouts with spinach and toasted almonds

Nuts

½ cup whole almonds, unpeeled

1 tablespoon peanut oil

1 teaspoon dark soy sauce

¼ teaspoon cayenne pepper

Salad

5 ounces (approx. 1 cup) mung bean
  or mixed sprouts

2 ounces alfalfa sprouts

extra virgin olive oil

1 tablespoon lemon juice

sea salt, black pepper

a few handfuls of young spinach leaves

Serves 4

Preheat the oven to 375°F. Toss the almonds in a bowl with the oil and soy sauce, then dust with the cayenne pepper and toss again. Tip the nuts into a small roasting or baking dish and spread them out in a single layer. Toast in the oven for 15–20 minutes, until deep golden and crisp. Transfer the nuts to a plate and leave to cool.

Place the mung bean or mixed sprouts and the alfalfa in a bowl and combine, teasing the alfalfa apart. Drizzle with 2 tablespoons of olive oil and ¾ tablespoon of lemon juice, season, and toss. Toss the spinach leaves in another bowl with a dash more oil, a squeeze of lemon, and a little seasoning. Divide the spinach between four plates and pile the sprouts on top. Scatter the almonds on top and serve.

There's nothing challenging in the way of textures here—the fried zucchini is as meltingly tender as the buffalo mozzarella, but given a little jolt by the mint and lemon.

salad of mozzarella, zucchini, lemon, and mint

extra virgin olive oil

4 medium zucchini, ends
   trimmed, sliced diagonally

sea salt, black pepper

2 buffalo mozzarellas, sliced

2 tablespoons fresh mint leaves

2 tablespoons lemon juice

Serves 4

You will probably need to cook the zucchini in two or three batches to avoid overcrowding the pan. Heat 2 tablespoons of olive oil in a large frying pan over medium heat, add some of the zucchini, season, and fry them for 4–5 minutes, turning them frequently, until translucent and starting to color, but remaining crisp. Don't worry if they haven't colored evenly.

Transfer them to a shallow serving dish (I use a 14-inch oval gratin dish), and cook the remainder in the same fashion, adding more oil to the pan as necessary. Leave the zucchini to cool. You can cook them several hours in advance, in which case cover and set aside in a cool place.

To finish assembling the salad, season the zucchini with a little more sea salt, then mix in the sliced mozzarella and mint. Whisk the lemon juice with 4 tablespoons of olive oil and pour it on top. Try to serve within 30–60 minutes.

The lightly boiled eggs and slivers of Parmesan turn this into a slightly more substantial salad that will serve as an appetizer or light lunch, but if you're serving it as one of a selection of salads or as an accompaniment you can leave them out.

salad of green beans with caper berries and parmesan

⅔ pound fine green beans, stalk ends
    trimmed
½ pound snow peas, stalk ends
    trimmed
4 medium eggs
4 purple (or green) scallions,
    trimmed and thinly sliced diagonally
6 tablespoons extra virgin olive oil
sea salt, black pepper
½ cup caper berries, stalks removed
2 ounces finely shaved Parmesan

Serves 4

Bring a large pot of salted water to a boil, add the green beans, and cook for 4 minutes, adding the snow peas after 2 minutes. Drain the vegetables into a colander, briefly run cold water through them to halt the cooking process, and set aside to cool.

In the meantime, bring a small pot of water to a boil and cook the eggs for 6 minutes. Drain them, then run cold water into the pot, and leave to cool completely.

Toss the beans, snow peas, and scallions with the olive oil in a bowl. (You can prepare the salad to this point in advance.) Shortly before serving, season the salad and toss in the caper berries. Divide the salad between four plates. Shell and halve the eggs and arrange them on top, then scatter the Parmesan on top.

A mélange of close relatives—snow peas, sugar snaps and peas—that all relish crisp salty bacon bits. White balsamic vinegar is gentle and sweet, and I grow fonder of it every time I use it, but you can play around with the dressing to suit your pantry.

pea, bacon, and pine nut salad

½ pound snow peas, stalk ends
   trimmed
½ pound sugar snaps, stalk ends
   trimmed
⅓ pound fresh shelled peas
½ pound bacon, diced
½ cup pine nuts
5 tablespoons avocado oil
2 tablespoons white balsamic vinegar
sea salt, black pepper
1 tablespoon coarsely chopped
   fresh tarragon
1 cup butter lettuce or bibb lettuce

Serves 6

Bring a large pot of salted water to a boil. Add the snow peas, sugar snaps, and peas, bring back to a boil, and cook for 2 minutes or until tender. Drain them into a colander and refresh under cold water, then leave to cool.

Heat a large frying pan over medium heat. Add the bacon, separating out the pieces, and fry for 4–5 minutes, until half-colored, stirring frequently. Add the pine nuts and fry for another 2–3 minutes, until both are golden, again stirring frequently. Use a slotted spoon to move to a double thickness of paper towel to drain and cool. You can prepare the recipe to this point an hour or two in advance.

Shortly before serving, toss the vegetables with the oil, vinegar, a pinch of salt, and some pepper, then fold in the bacon and pine nuts, the tarragon and the lettuce.

Frozen baby fava beans are one of the best finds in the freezer aisle. It would take you a long time to amass this number from a mountain of pods, but if it happens to be early enough in the season, before their skins toughen, fresh would be a treat.

fava bean and feta salad

1 pound frozen baby fava beans

extra virgin olive oil

juice of ½ lemon

sea salt, black pepper

3 scallions, trimmed
and finely sliced diagonally

6 tablespoons coarsely chopped
fresh flat-leaf parsley

7 ounces feta, crumbled

a handful of arugula leaves (optional)

Serves 4–6

Bring a large pot of water to a boil and cook the fava beans according to the package instructions. Drain into a colander and leave for a few minutes for the water to evaporate. Toss the hot beans in a bowl with the 6 tablespoons of olive oil, the lemon juice, and some seasoning and leave to cool.

Toss in the scallions and two-thirds of the parsley. Scatter the feta and remaining parsley over the top and splash with a little more oil. The salad is good to eat for some time, but it will absorb the dressing after several hours so you may want to add a little more oil just before serving. You can also toss a few arugula leaves into the salad or serve it scattered over a few dressed leaves.

Both baby romanesco cauliflowers and fennel have an even better texture in their nascent state than when they are larger. Carrots too should be on the thin side in the name of delicacy. The anchovies here could just as well be olives.

caponata of summer vegetables

5 tablespoons extra virgin olive oil

⅓ pound each of cauliflower or
  romanesco florets, broccoli florets,
  young carrots (peeled, halved, and
  cut into 1 inch lengths), yellow or
  green beans (stalk ends trimmed,
  halved), fennel segments or baby
  fennel (halved)

1 bunch of scallions, trimmed
  and halved

⅔ cup white wine

sea salt, black pepper

juice of ½ lemon

6 anchovy fillets in oil,
  halved lengthways

2 tablespoons capers, rinsed

3 tablespoons coarsely chopped
  fresh flat-leaf parsley

Serves 4

Heat 2 tablespoons of the olive oil in a large saucepan over medium heat, then add all the vegetables and sweat for about 5 minutes until they begin to color, stirring occasionally. Add the wine and some seasoning, cover the pan, and cook over low heat for 5 minutes or until just tender, but with a little resistance. Transfer the vegetables to a bowl and reduce the residual liquor to a couple of tablespoons. Pour this over the vegetables and leave them to cool.

To finish the caponata, pour the lemon juice and remaining olive oil on top. Toss in the anchovies, capers, and parsley, and season to taste.

This idiosyncratic salad comes from a favorite book, *Real Greek Food*, by Theodore Kyriakou and Charles Campion. It's almost too tempting not to serve some fried halloumi and oily black olives alongside.

salad of green peppers and peaches

2 pounds green peppers

8 tablespoons extra virgin olive oil

1 level tablespoon brown sugar

sea salt, black pepper

3 large ripe (but not over-ripe) peaches
   or nectarines

½ tablespoon cumin seeds

¼ teaspoon cayenne pepper

½ tablespoon lemon juice

Serves 4

Preheat the oven to 375°F. Remove the core and seeds from the green peppers and quarter them. Arrange them in a roasting dish, drizzle with half the olive oil, scatter the sugar on top, and season well. Roast for 45–60 minutes, giving them a stir halfway through to ensure they caramelize evenly. Remove and leave to cool.

If you are feeling fastidious you can peel the peaches or nectarines—plunge them into a pan of boiling water for 30 seconds, then into a sink of cold water, and slip off the skins using a knife to assist. Slice them into wedges and slip out the stone. Place the slices in a salad bowl and mix in the green peppers and any juices in the bottom of the pan.

Heat the cumin seeds in a small frying pan over medium heat until they begin to smell fragrant, tossing them constantly. Crush them using a pestle and mortar, then combine with the cayenne pepper and a little salt, and toss this into the salad. Add the remaining olive oil and lemon juice and toss again. Check the seasoning and serve.

small salads

These salads are united in size, and will play supporting roles beside whatever small cuts look good at the butcher or fishmonger. The lead is a very simple tomato salad, something I tend to make as a matter of course with almost every dinner. I buy tomatoes throughout the week, especially during the summer months, gathering different varieties wherever I'm shopping to top up the "tomato bowl," which at its best is every bit as showy as the fruit bowl. Like a green salad, a plate of lightly seasoned sliced tomatoes has the ability to go with pretty much whatever you serve it with. It's that balance of sweet and sour that always seem to provide the missing note, and get along with everything.

Coleslaw is another classic favorite, delicious with fried chicken scallopines touched with mustard or a flank steak with garlic butter, but here it's made with Savoy cabbage, that tad lighter than the norm of thick strands of white cabbage. A celeriac remoulade is also a great all-rounder, and particularly good with a selection of cheese at lunchtime.

And then there are a couple of little salads that rely on cans of beans. If, however, you come across fresh or semi-dried beans in their pods, such as the French "coco" or haricot beans, these cook up to creamy tenderness in about twenty minutes. A package of button mushrooms is also a good staple to pop into the basket on the way around the supermarket. Finely sliced, they make the most delicate of side salads.

Tomatoes would be my desert island vegetable. A plate of sliced tomatoes on the table is as standard in our house as a green salad. And even when it's not called for, it's a very good reason for getting out the cheese afterwards and wiping the plate clean of juices with a crust of bread. Although that in itself can become a bad habit—I hate to think how many calories I've consumed over the years grazing on what amounts to a second dinner.

a gorgeous tomato salad

1½ pounds assorted tomatoes, e.g.
   cherry, plum, and beefsteak

¾ teaspoon sea salt

½ teaspoon superfine sugar

a handful of fresh green or purple basil
   leaves, torn

6 tablespoons extra virgin olive oil

Serves 4

Cherry tomatoes excepted, cut out the core from the tomatoes. Halve, quarter or slice the tomatoes as seems appropriate; a serrated knife is good for this. Arrange on a large plate, sprinkle with the salt and sugar, and leave for 30 minutes. Sprinkle with basil and drizzle the olive oil on top.

Crisp strips of bacon are especially good with the sweet tartness of the apple, which in turn is especially good with celeriac, but vegetarians can turn to dates or some nice plump prunes as an alternative.

apple and celeriac remoulade

Remoulade

1 celeriac bulb (approx. 1¾ pound), peeled

1 level teaspoon sea salt

12 strips bacon

1 red-skinned apple, quartered, cored, and thinly sliced lengthways

1 tablespoon lemon juice

4 tablespoons coarsely chopped fresh flat-leaf parsley, plus a little extra to serve

Mayonnaise

1 large organic egg yolk

2 tablespoons Dijon mustard

1 cup peanut oil

1 tablespoon lemon juice

Serves 6

Finely grate the celeriac. Toss it with the sea salt in a large bowl and leave for 20 minutes. Heat the broiler, lay the strips of bacon on the grid of a broiler pan, and cook either side until golden and crisp.

Whisk the egg yolk and mustard together in a bowl, then whisk in the oil, very slowly to begin with until the mayonnaise takes, then in slightly bolder streams. Whisk in the lemon juice. It will be a little thinner than a normal mayonnaise.

Place the celeriac in batches in a clean kitchen towel and wring out as much liquid as possible—this should rid it of any browning juices. Return it to the bowl and tease the lumps with your fingers to unravel the strands. Add the mayonnaise and blend with a wooden spoon. Toss the apple with the lemon juice and mix into the celeriac with the parsley. Transfer the salad to a clean bowl and scatter with a little extra parsley.

Serve the remoulade with a slice or two of bacon draped on top. The remoulade can also be made several hours in advance, in which case cover and chill until required, bringing it back to room temperature 30 minutes before serving.

Even though coleslaw is classically made using white cabbage, I prefer Savoy, which is that much more delicate and leafy. But here, as with any coleslaw, fineness is everything, so sharpen up that vegetable knife before starting.

savoy coleslaw

1 heaping tablespoon sesame seeds

1 Savoy cabbage, tough outer leaves removed

2 teaspoons Dijon mustard

1½ cups sour cream

½ teaspoon superfine sugar

sea salt, black pepper

⅓ cup currants

3 tablespoons coarsely chopped fresh cilantro leaves, plus a little extra to serve

Serves 6

Heat a large frying pan over medium heat and toast the sesame seeds until golden, stirring occasionally. Transfer them to a bowl and leave to cool.

Quarter the cabbage, remove the core, slice as finely as possible, and place in a large bowl.

To make the dressing, blend the mustard with the sour cream, then add the sugar and some seasoning. Toss the cabbage with the dressing, then mix in the currants and cilantro leaves. Transfer to a serving plate or bowl, and scatter the sesame seeds and a little more cilantro on top. You can prepare the salad up to a couple of hours in advance, in which case cover and set aside in a cool place.

fruit 'n' feta

feta, pomegranate, and hazelnut salad

Full of clean, crisp flavors, especially good around Christmas when your palate's dozed off after all the rich seasonal fare.

½ cup hazelnuts, cut in half

seeds of 3 pomegranates

14 ounces feta, cut into ½-inch dice

3 handfuls of fresh flat-leaf
  parsley leaves

4 tablespoons extra virgin olive oil

1 tablespoon lemon juice

black pepper

Serves 6

Preheat the oven to 375°F. Lay the hazelnuts in a single layer on a small baking tray and toast in the oven for 10 minutes until golden. Remove and leave them to cool.

Put the pomegranate seeds in a bowl and add the feta, hazelnuts, and parsley. Pour the olive oil and lemon juice on top, and add a grinding of black pepper. Very gently toss to combine the ingredients. You can prepare this salad a couple of hours in advance.

orange, feta, and herb salad

Here cubes of feta sit marinating in olive oil and lemon juice before being acquainted with a leafy mass of herbs and juicy orange segments. The ingredients are layered, so you can make it well in advance and toss it at the last minute.

2 oranges

14 ounces feta, cut into ½-inch dice

6 tablespoons extra virgin olive oil

1½ tablespoons lemon juice

1 red onion, peeled, halved, and finely sliced

1¼ cups mixture of fresh mint, cilantro, and flat-leaf parsley leaves

Serves 4

Cut the skin and outer pith off the oranges. Thinly slice them crosswise, then into quarters.

Put the feta in the bottom of a large deep salad bowl and pour the olive oil and lemon juice on top. Scatter the onion on top, separating out the strands. Next arrange the herb leaves in a layer, and finally scatter the orange on top. Cover with plastic wrap and set aside in a cool place until ready to eat.

Just before eating, plunge a couple of spoons into the bottom of the bowl and gently toss the salad, turning it just a few times to avoid breaking the feta up.

Fresh pulses are such a treat, sweet and creamy with none of the dry chalkiness that so often characterises dried pulses. Would they were more readily available— snap them up when you come across them, and cook them as below.

borlotti bean, red onion, and tomato salad

4 plum tomatoes

12 ounces canned borlotti or cannellini beans, rinsed*

1 small red onion, peeled, halved, and thinly sliced

5 tablespoons coarsely chopped fresh flat-leaf parsley

6 tablespoons extra virgin olive oil

1 tablespoon lemon juice

sea salt, black pepper

Serves 4

Bring a small pot of water to a boil. Cut out a cone from the top of each tomato, plunge them first into the boiling water for 20 seconds, then into cold water. Slip off the skins, quarter, discarding the seeds, then dice the remaining flesh.

Combine the borlotti beans, red onion, diced tomato, and parsley in a bowl. Pour the olive oil and lemon juice on top and toss, then season to taste with salt and pepper.

*For fresh beans, place in a shallow ovenproof container. Cover with water by 1 inch, then add about 5 unpeeled garlic cloves, a sprig of fresh rosemary, a bay leaf, and a halved tomato. Pour over 2 tablespoons of olive oil, cover with foil, and bake for 1–2 hours at 375°F until tender. Leave them to cool in the water.

This is a good salad for a picnic, when it's nice to have something raw and crunchy. And it's not too hearty—the vegetables are very finely sliced and soften after marinating in olive oil.

fennel, carrot, and radish salad with olives

1 fennel bulb, trimmed and outer
   sheath discarded, halved and
   finely sliced

6 radishes, trimmed and finely sliced

2 slim carrots, trimmed, peeled, and
   finely sliced

½ red onion, peeled and finely sliced

½ cup green and black olives,
   pitted and finely sliced

3 tablespoons extra virgin olive oil

1 teaspoon balsamic vinegar

sea salt, black pepper

Serves 6

Combine all the vegetables and the olives in a shallow dish, and toss with the olive oil and vinegar. Season the salad just before serving—if you do this in advance the salt will draw the juices out of the vegetables and they'll lose their freshness. Cover and leave in a cool place.

Lovers of Russian salad will favor this one, a mixture of fava and green beans in a light tarragon mayonnaise. Some quail's eggs or cooked tail-on shrimp would be good in its company.

beans in mayonnaise

¾ pound fine green beans,
   stalk ends trimmed, halved
½ pound fresh or frozen fava beans
1 organic egg yolk
½ teaspoon Dijon mustard
a squeeze of lemon juice
½ cup peanut oil
sea salt, black pepper
1 teaspoon chopped fresh tarragon

Serves 4–6

Bring two medium pots of salted water to a boil. Add the green beans to one of the pots and cook for 2–3 minutes until just tender, then immerse in a sink of cold water to cool. Add the fava beans to the other, and simmer for 3–4 minutes if frozen, 6 minutes if fresh. Drain, leave to cool, and then peel them.

Whisk the egg yolk with the mustard and the lemon juice. Gradually whisk in the peanut oil, then thin with a drop of water, season, and add a little chopped tarragon. Toss with the beans.

This Moroccan salad will grace any line-up of mezze, with some dips and warmed mini flatbreads, cocktail gherkins, or other pickles and olives. And it's particularly good with feta.

carrot and cumin salad

1½ pounds bunched carrots, trimmed, peeled, halved lengthways if large, and sliced diagonally

6 tablespoons extra virgin olive oil

1 teaspoon cumin seeds, coarsely ground

1 garlic clove, peeled and crushed to a paste

sea salt

a generous squeeze of lemon juice

a few handfuls of arugula leaves to serve

Serves 6

Bring a medium pot of salted water to a boil, add the carrots, and simmer for 5 minutes or until just tender. Drain into a colander or sieve, leave to steam dry for a few minutes, then place in a bowl. Dress with the olive oil, cumin, garlic, some salt, and a generous squeeze of lemon juice to taste. Leave to cool. Shortly before serving, toss a pile of arugula leaves into the salad.

green salads

A beautiful green salad is one of the benchmarks of home cooking. For some it is how you poach an egg that reveals the kind of cook you are, whereas for me it is how you toss a pile of green salad leaves.

That said, it doesn't help that so many salad greens are now sold in lifeless plastic pouches. Even at their very freshest, to prepare a decent salad with these is never going to be more than a salvage operation. By the time you have cut off the browning edges and cherry-picked the tender leaf from the tough stalk, you would have done better to start with a whole lettuce or head of leaves. Big blowsy escaroles, mop-headed frisées, and crisp heads of Romaine are a treat. And in their absence, Little Gem hearts are nearly always available. Those floppy English lettuces that could have been pencil-drawn in a Beatrix Potter sketch are also not to be sniffed at.

You can plump them out with mustard greens, arugula, and watercress, the latter ideally bought by the bunch to guarantee its maturity and sharp peppery flavor. Butter lettuce or mâche too is at its best bought with its whiskery roots attached and traces of the soil it grew in. Some or any of these make a fine start, with a few slivers of scallion to spice them up—the selection of these gets better and better, ranging in size from pencil-slim to buxom beauties in shades of purple as well as green.

And so to the dressing. It's worth making up a generous-sized jar of vinaigrette, and having a stock favorite formula that's personal to you. The one that follows has a little bit of everything I like to find in a salad dressing—some Dijon mustard, sugar, and a hint of garlic, and not too much olive oil, just enough to let its presence be felt. Thick dressings with thin leaves are also particularly alluring—a dollop of green goddess mayo or some homemade salad cream.

This is the kind of green salad that has us coming back for more, though it doesn't have to feature this many types of green leaf. If it's supper for two at home, you may well just want to run to the one type, while the dressing is a great basic and worth adapting to your taste to make up in quantity.

a gorgeous green salad

Dressing

1 tablespoon red wine vinegar

½ teaspoon wholegrain mustard

½ teaspoon Dijon mustard

½ garlic clove, peeled and crushed to
   a paste

1 teaspoon superfine sugar

sea salt, black pepper

2 tablespoons extra virgin olive oil

5 tablespoons peanut oil

Salad

1 Romaine lettuce heart, damaged
   leaves discarded, sliced ½ inch thick

a handful or two of butter lettuce

a handful or two of watercress sprigs

½ container of mustard greens

2 scallions, thinly sliced

Serves 4

Whisk the vinegar, mustards, garlic, sugar, and seasoning in a bowl, then gradually whisk in the oils until you have a light emulsified dressing.

Toss the Romaine lettuce, butter lettuce, and watercress in a large salad bowl, and scatter the mustard greens and scallions in the center. Toss with the dressing just before serving.

Oh-so pretty, a selection of crisp lettuce hearts and micro leaves. These perfectly formed miniatures consist of the cotyledon (the first two leaves to shoot), and the first true leaves below, and they stop you mid-forkful by dint of their sheer daintiness, they are also beautifully tender. But don't be boxed in by the selection—if you can't find micro leaves, tear some ordinary herbs into pieces. Pea shoots, however, are at last ubiquitous.

lettuce heart and little leaf salad

Dressing

1 medium organic egg yolk
1 teaspoon Dijon mustard
½ cup avocado oil, plus 2 tablespoons
a squeeze of lemon juice, plus
    1 tablespoon
sea salt

Salad

2 green Little Gem hearts
1 red Little Gem heart
2 small heads of red chicory
a few pinches of sprouts, e.g. alfalfa
    and radish
a small handful of pea shoots
4 tablespoons fresh micro herbs,
    e.g. basil and cilantro
4 breakfast radishes, trimmed and
    finely sliced

Serves 4

Make the dressing close to the time of serving to avoid it separating—it should be the consistency of a thin mayonnaise. Whisk the egg yolk with the mustard in a bowl, then slowly whisk in ½ cup of avocado oil a few drops at a time to begin with until the dressing emulsifies. Add a squeeze of lemon juice.

Trim the base of the lettuce hearts and chicory, discarding any damaged outer leaves. Cut the red chicory and red Little Gem heart into quarters or thin segments, and slice the green Little Gem hearts across. Gently toss these in a bowl with 1 tablespoon of lemon juice, 2 tablespoons of avocado oil, and a little salt and arrange on a large serving plate. Place a few pinches of sprouts here and there. Drizzle with about two-thirds of the dressing, reserving the rest for some other use. Scatter the pea shoots, micro herbs, and radishes on top.

The stuff of dreamy delis—flat, squeaky-crisp roasted Marcona almonds, juicy raisins, and sheep's or goat's milk cheese just beginning to ooze below the rind. In fact Little Gems have never seemed more glam.

little gem, almond, and raisin salad

2 Little Gem hearts, trimmed
   and leaves separated
5 ounces thin slices of soft or semi-soft
   sheep's or goat's milk cheese
canola or extra virgin olive oil
a squeeze of lemon juice
a pinch of sea salt
⅓ cup roasted, salted Marcona
   almonds
⅓ cup raisins
2 scallions, trimmed
   and thinly sliced

Serves 4

Arrange the leaves from the Little Gem hearts on a large plate with the cheese. Drizzle with some oil, squeeze a little lemon juice over, and season with a pinch of salt, then scatter the almonds, raisins, and scallions on top.

The French, with astute rationale, serve cheese before dessert, hence avoiding the confusion of going from savory to sweet and back again, which wreaks havoc with the wines. But more than this, a small salad with the cheese course does away with filling up on cookies at a stage of the meal when the last thing you feel like is another dose of carbs. The dressing is that little bit tarter than most vinaigrettes, which usually contain a generous hit of sugar to soothe the vinegar.

green salad for cheese

Salad
salad greens for 6 small green salads,
   e.g. escarole, butter lettuce, Little
   Gem leaves, or a mixture

Dressing
2 teaspoons sherry vinegar
a squeeze of lemon juice
½ teaspoon Dijon mustard
sea salt, black pepper
1 teaspoon finely chopped shallot
½ garlic clove, peeled, finely chopped
3 tablespoons extra virgin olive oil

Serves 6

Whisk the vinegar and lemon juice with the mustard and seasoning in a bowl. Add the shallot and garlic and the oil.

Just before serving toss the leaves with the dressing in a bowl.

This salad is mainly an excuse to eat a large plate of very fine smoked salmon, with the cucumber yogurt a civilized intermediary between the two.

peppery salad with cucumber yogurt

1 cucumber

sea salt

½ teaspoon superfine sugar

5 ounces (approx. ⅔ cup) Greek yogurt

juice of ¼ lemon

3 scallions, trimmed and finely sliced

1 pound smoked salmon (optional)

black pepper

mixture of arugula, watercress, and
    mustard and cress, to feed 4

peanut oil

Serves 4

Trim the ends off the cucumber and peel it. Quarter it lengthways and cut out the seeds. Cut each quarter into thin strips, then slice these into 1-inch lengths. Place the cucumber in a bowl and toss with ½ teaspoon of salt and the sugar. Leave for 30 minutes to exude its juices, then drain in a sieve, rinse thoroughly under cold water, and pat dry on a kitchen towel. Mix the cucumber in a bowl with the yogurt, a squeeze of lemon juice, and half the scallion.

Lay out the smoked salmon (if using) on four plates and grind over a little black pepper. Toss the greens in a bowl with enough oil to coat, then add a few drops of lemon juice, and the smallest pinch of sea salt. Place a pile of greens on the plates, with a pile of cucumber salad. Scatter over the remaining scallion.

My green credentials desert me when it comes to green beans—in the dark, snowy depths of winter, wafer-fine beans are that little bit too hard to resist even though they do come from the other side of the world.

chunky green salad

½ pound fine green beans,
   stalk ends trimmed
1 medium zucchini (approx. ½ pound),
   trimmed and very finely sliced
¼ red onion, finely sliced
juice of 1 lemon
extra virgin olive oil
sea salt, black pepper
2 avocados (ideally Hass)
2 bunches of mustard greens
2 ounces finely sliced Parmesan

Serves 4

Bring a large pot of salted water to a boil and cook the beans for 3–4 minutes until just tender. Transfer to a sink of cold water, using a slotted spoon. Once cool, remove and drain on a kitchen towel.

Toss the zucchini, beans, and red onion in a salad bowl with the lemon juice, 3 tablespoons of olive oil, and some seasoning. Quarter the avocados and remove the stone, then peel off the skin and cut into long thin slices. Carefully fold these into the salad, then gently toss in the mustard greens. Pile on to plates, scatter with the Parmesan, and drizzle a little more oil on top.

We've cut out the guilty bits here—the eggs and Parmesan—and baked the croutons for a lighter Caesar. But given that anchovies never went terribly well with cheese in the first place, it's no bad thing. Though you can always serve Parmesan on the side for those who can't live without it.

caesar salad "lite"

4 thin slices of sourdough bread, crusts removed, cut to approx. ½ inch dice
8 tablespoons extra virgin olive oil
½ teaspoon dried oregano
sea salt, black pepper
1 tablespoon lemon juice
1 teaspoon Worcestershire sauce
1 small garlic clove, peeled and crushed
2 Romaine hearts
2 avocados (ideally Hass)
6 salted anchovy fillets, halved lengthways
3 tablespoons snipped fresh chives

Serves 4–6

Preheat the oven to 400°F. Toss the bread cubes with 1 tablespoon of olive oil, the oregano, and a pinch of salt. Scatter them over a baking sheet and toast in the oven for 9–11 minutes until light gold. Leave to cool.

To make the dressing, whisk the lemon juice, Worcestershire sauce, garlic, and some seasoning in a small bowl, then whisk in the remaining oil.

Separate out the leaves from the lettuces and cut them into chunky pieces. Quarter the avocados and remove the stone, then peel off the skin, and cut into long thin slices. Combine the lettuce, avocado, anchovies, and chives in a large shallow dish or bowl. Pour over the dressing and scatter the croutons on top.

Frisée lettuces can vary hugely in size, so if it's an enormous blowsy affair use enough leaves for four and reserve the remainder for another salad. Dark green and tough outside leaves needn't go to waste— they're a delight wilted in olive oil with a little garlic and chile, their bitterness receding into the distance as they are heated.

farmer's market salad

Salad

1 frisée lettuce

¼ pound fine green beans, stalk ends trimmed and halved

6 large cherry tomatoes, cut into wedges

⅓ pound bacon

2 thick slices of pain de Campagne or coarse-textured white bread, cut into ½-inch dice

Dressing

1 tablespoon Dijon mustard

2 teaspoons red wine vinegar

sea salt

3 tablespoons peanut oil

Serves 4

The best way to prepare a frisée lettuce is to hold it by the stalk and give it a radical trim around the edges, removing several inches of the dark green leaves at the top which are tough and bitter to eat. Now cut out the stalk and discard the periphery of outer leaves. Separate and tear up the remaining pale green fronds and wash them in a sink of cold water. Shake or spin them dry and place them in a large salad bowl. Bring a small pot of salted water to a boil, add the beans, and simmer for 3–4 minutes, leaving them firm to the bite. Drain and refresh them in cold water, then toss them into the leaves with the tomatoes.

To make the dressing, whisk the mustard with the vinegar and some sea salt in a small bowl, then whisk in the oil.

Heat a frying pan over medium-low heat and fry the bacon for about 4 minutes, stirring occasionally. Add the bread to the pan and continue to cook for another 4 minutes, tossing frequently, until the bacon is frazzled and crisp and the bread has started to toast at the edges. Toss the salad with the dressing. Distribute the contents of the pan over the top of the salad, toss it, and serve immediately, while the bacon and croutons are warm.

The heartstone here is those quintessential English salad ingredients that we love to smother in salad cream—boiled eggs, floppy green lettuce leaves, radishes, and scallions. If you have the English country garden to eat it in, so much the better.

english country garden salad

Salad Cream

3 medium egg yolks

4 tablespoons heavy cream

1 teaspoon English mustard

1 teaspoon superfine sugar

1 tablespoon white wine vinegar

sea salt

Salad

12 quail's eggs

2 floppy green lettuces

2 handfuls long radishes, trimmed

4 scallions, trimmed and thinly
   sliced diagonally

2 tablespoons coarsely snipped
   fresh chives

Serves 6

Whisk all the ingredients for the salad cream in a bowl set over a pan with a little simmering water in it, then stir constantly for a few minutes until it thickens, taking care not to overheat it otherwise it will scramble. Pass the salad cream through a sieve into a bowl, cover the surface with plastic wrap, leave to cool, then chill until required.

Bring a small pan of water to a boil and carefully lower in the quail's eggs. Cook for 2½ minutes, then drain, refill the pan with cold water, and leave to cool. Shell the eggs by pinching a little of the shell and gently pulling to remove it.

Twist the base off the lettuces, discard the leathery outer leaves, and without separating the remainder rinse the lettuce under cold water inside and out. Thoroughly shake the lettuces dry and then place each one in a bowl, opening out the leaves as though they were a flower. Scatter the radishes, scallions, and eggs on top. The salads can be prepared to this point in advance, in which case cover and set aside.

Just before serving, spoon the salad cream over the salads and scatter the chives on top.

White balsamic vinegar is a relative newcomer on the block, and altogether different from the dark kind. It's delicate, sweet and sour, and great in salads that call for a little sharpening without the full-on acidity of a wine vinegar. Avocado oil too is relatively new, but seems here to stay, and has a real taste of the fruit itself. But as ever, oils and vinegars are open to whatever largesse your pantry is offering up.

salad of baby spinach, avocado, and dates

1 tablespoon white balsamic vinegar

sea salt, black pepper

4 tablespoons avocado oil

1 cup Greek-style yogurt

a pinch of saffron filaments (about 20), ground and infused with 1 teaspoon boiling water

2 avocados (ideally Hass)

5 ounces baby spinach

1 cup Medjool dates, stoned and cut into long thin strips

¼ cup walnut pieces

Serves 4–6

Whisk the vinegar with some seasoning in a bowl, then whisk in the oil. Blend the yogurt with the saffron infusion and a little salt in another bowl. The two dressings can be prepared in advance, in which case cover and chill the yogurt.

Quarter the avocados and remove from the stone, then peel off the skin and cut the flesh into long thin strips. Toss the spinach leaves with the vinaigrette in a large bowl or shallow serving dish, then mix in the avocado and dates. Scatter the walnuts on top, and serve as soon as possible with the bowl of yogurt on the side.

rich dressings

These lie on the other side of the fence from vinaigrettes, thick and unctuous, for dolloping on chunky, Romaine, and Little Gem leaves, though there's nothing to stop you dressing them with a vinaigrette first. Some will also serve as a little sauce for grilled meat or fish, and are good for dipping too.

green goddess mayo

This belongs to the Martini era. Slather it over halves of boiled egg, dish it up with a bowl of lightly cooked quail's eggs, or spread it over warm blinis with some smoked salmon, or salmon roe and snipped chives.

⅔ cup Hellmann's mayonnaise
1 scallion, trimmed and chopped
2 tablespoons chopped fresh cilantro leaves
2 tablespoons chopped fresh basil leaves
1 teaspoon chopped fresh tarragon leaves

Serves 4

Place all the ingredients in the bowl of a food processor and blend to a green sauce. Transfer to a bowl, cover, and chill until required.

easy salad cream

Quicker than the real thing (see page 183), this is basically Heinz with a little bit of help. For a simple salad arrange four trimmed and quartered Little Gem lettuces on four plates, with a few trimmed radishes and a halved scallion on each, and drizzle the dressing over.

3 tablespoons Heinz salad cream
3 tablespoons light cream or low-fat yogurt
½ teaspoon English mustard

Serves 4

Blend together all the ingredients for the salad cream in a bowl, cover, and chill until required.

garlic yogurt dressing

Creamy but not overly rich, dollop this over Romaine leaves and scatter with slivers of green or purple scallions.

1½ cups creamy yogurt
pinch of superfine sugar
sea salt
1 garlic clove, peeled and crushed to a paste
2 tablespoons extra virgin olive oil

Serves 4–6

Blend all the ingredients for the dressing together in a bowl. You can make this well in advance, in which case cover and chill it.

deviled english dressing

This gorgeous sunny yellow dressing sports wholly English credentials, being made with rapeseed oil. It's a green option for all those in England who want to cook and eat ingredients produced close to home.

1 tablespoon cider vinegar
2 teaspoons Colman's English mustard
1 scant teaspoon superfine sugar
sea salt
7 tablespoons rapeseed or canola oil

Serves 4

Whisk the vinegar, mustard, sugar, and a little salt together in a medium bowl, then gradually whisk in the oil a tablespoon or two at a time until the dressing emulsifies—it should by the end be thick and dark yellow. If necessary give it another whisk before using, to emulsify it again.

walnut and garlic dressing

This feisty Balkan dressing is good cold-weather stuff as well as hot, and you could serve it with some cooked veggies or cold roast chicken, and salad greens.

1 slice of white bread, crusts removed
1 garlic clove, peeled
approx. ½ cup shelled walnuts
2 tablespoons walnut oil
a squeeze of lemon juice
½ teaspoon sea salt
½ teaspoon superfine sugar
3 heaping tablespoons Greek yogurt

Serves 4

Briefly soak the bread in water and then squeeze it out using your hands. Blend together the garlic clove, walnuts, bread, walnut oil, lemon juice, sea salt, and sugar. Add the Greek yogurt and blend. Cover and chill until required.

index

acknowledgments

With many thanks to Angela Mason, to my agent Rosemary Sandberg, to Suzanna de Jong, Editor, Annie Lee, Copy Editor, and to Kyle Cathie. And with love and thanks to Jonnie, Rothko, and Louis.